BK-308

"Say and Do®"

Positive Pragma...

Game Boards

Fun Sheets

A Companion Book to the "Say and Do®" Positive Pragmatic Game Boards

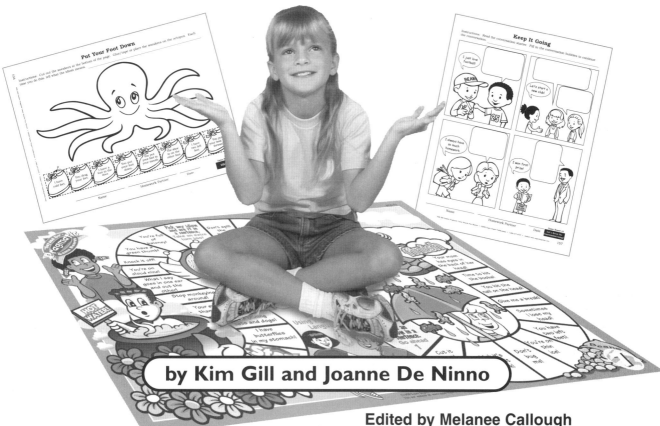

by Kim Gill and Joanne De Ninno

Edited by Melanee Callough
Illustrated by Bruce Ink

Post Office Box 24997, Greenville, South Carolina 29616
Call Toll Free 1-800-277-8737 • Fax Toll Free 1-800-978-7379
Online! www.superduperinc.com
E-Mail: custserv@superduperinc.com

ISBN 1-58650-352-9

Dedication

This book is dedicated to

Karen Antignano

and

Linda Cohen

who have created an environment where

all children are encouraged and inspired

to learn and to communicate freely.

#BK-308 Positive Pragmatic Game Boards Fun Sheets • ©2003 Super Duper® Publications • 1-800-277-8737 • Online! www.superduperinc.com

Introduction

"Say and Do®" Positive Pragmatic Game Boards Fun Sheets is a reproducible book designed to accompany Super Duper®'s *"Say and Do®" Positive Pragmatic Game Boards*. The activity pages target a variety of social language goals:

Let's Give Information - The child explains how to sequence an activity.

Talk Me Into It - The child uses language to convince or persuade.

What Would You Ask? - The child asks questions in order to obtain more information.

It's Telephone Time - The child develops appropriate skills for telephone use.

What Should You Do? - The child interprets situations in order to solve problems.

Feelings - The child interprets and expresses emotions.

What Do These Really Mean? - The child interprets and explains commonly used idioms.

What Should You Do Instead Of...? - The child recognizes and corrects inappropriate behaviors.

What Would You Say? - The child uses appropriate greetings, farewells and various politeness forms.

Let's Keep the Conversation Going - The child takes conversational turns given a specific topic.

To use the *Positive Pragmatic Fun Sheets*, simply choose the sheets that correspond to the game board and goal you have selected for your language session. The sheets will appeal to children of varying interests, chronological ages, and language levels. Use the Fun Sheets as an introduction, follow-up to the game boards, or as homework assignments to reinforce target objectives.

Each chapter includes activity sheets for each game board, providing an opportunity for plenty of practice for your students. The sheets incorporate the situations presented on the game boards, as well as many new situations. This will assist your students in applying his/her new skills to a variety of everyday settings and experiences.

The materials are ready to use with minimal preparation for both individual and group therapy or homework. The book includes a variety of games, coloring, cut and paste pages, fill-ins, role-playing, puzzles, stories, and other exciting activities. Your students will enjoy reaching their pragmatic language goals with - *"Say and Do®" Positive Pragmatic Game Boards* and *"Say and Do®" Positive Pragmatic Game Boards Fun Sheets*. Teachers, therapists, parents, and students will have fun working, learning and communicating together!

Table of Contents

Table of Contents

Parent/Helper Letter

Date:_____

Dear Parent/Homework Helper:

   Your child is currently working on _____
to help improve his/her social skills. You can help your child's
progress by completing the attached activity sheet.

☐ Please sign the worksheet in the designated spot and return it to
   me by _____.

☐ Please complete this sheet at home. You do not need to return it.

   Have fun helping your child develop his/her social skills!

   Thank you,

_____
            Name

_____
      Parent/Helper's Signature

Game Board 1

Let's Give Information

Tell How To...

Number the Sequence

Instructions: Cut out the numbers at the bottom of the page. Glue/tape or place the numbers 1-3 below each picture to indicate the correct story order. Tell how to complete each task step by step. (Complete each title, too!) _____

1. How to _____

2. How to _____

1	2	3	1	2	3

_____ _____ _____

Name   Homework Partner   Date

Game Board 1

Let's Give Information

"How To" Sequence

Instructions: Cut out the pictures at the bottom of the page. Glue, tape or place each picture in the correct order. Write or say a sentence to describe each picture. Tell how to complete each task step by step!

How To Make A Bed

1	2	3

_____
_____
_____

How To Make An Ice Cream Sundae

1	2	3

_____
_____
_____

_____   _____   _____

Name   Homework Partner   Date

Let's Give Information

Game Board 1

"What Happens Before" Listening

Instructions: Read/listen to each sentence below. Color or circle the correct picture that completes each sentence. Say the sentence aloud. As a bonus, write your answer.

1. Before you plant flower seeds, you must...

_____.

2. Before you catch a fish, you must...

_____.

3. Before you eat a sandwich, you must...

_____.

4. Before you play at the beach, you must...

_____.

_____   _____   _____   **Game Board 1**

Name   Homework Partner   Date

Let's Give Information

   #BK-308 Positive Pragmatic Game Boards Fun Sheets • ©2003 Super Duper® Publications • 1-800-277-8737 • Online! www.superduperinc.com

"What Happens After" Listening

Instructions: Read/listen to each sentence below. Color or circle the correct picture that completes each sentence. Say the sentence aloud. As a bonus, write your answer.

1. After you wrap a present, you can...

_____.

2. After you rake the leaves, you must...

_____.

3. After you build a snowman, you can...

_____.

4. After you get ready for school, you will...

_____.

First, Next, Last

Instructions: Look at the three pictures. Number each picture in the correct order. Say and/or write a sentence about each picture. Use the words "first," "next," and "last."

First, _____.

Next, _____.

Last, _____.

First, _____.

Next, _____.

Last, _____.

_____   _____   _____

Name   Homework Partner   Date

Game Board 1

Let's Give Information

#BK-308 Positive Pragmatic Game Boards Fun Sheets • ©2003 Super Duper® Publications • 1-800-277-8737 • Online! www.superduperinc.com

What's in the Middle?

Instructions: Draw what happens in the middle box below. Then, use the pictures and tell what happened in all three boxes of each scene. _____

1.

2.

3.

4.

Name   Homework Partner   Date

Game Board 1

Let's Give Information

#BK-308 Positive Pragmatic Game Boards Fun Sheets • ©2003 Super Duper® Publications • 1-800-277-8737 • Online! www.superduperinc.com

7

Fill in the Missing Step

Instructions: Look at the three boxes in each row. Draw, write, or say what is missing in the sequence. Tell about all three steps. _____

Name _____ Homework Partner _____ Date _____

Let's Give Information

#BK-308 Positive Pragmatic Game Boards Fun Sheets • ©2003 Super Duper® Publications • 1-800-277-8737 • Online! www.superduperinc.com

The Last Step

Instructions: Look at the two pictures. Tell what is happening in each one. On the line, draw, write, or say the last step (or steps!) in each sequence.

_____

_____

_____

_____

Listen and Say

Instructions: Read/listen to the two sentences. Repeat the two sentences in the correct order. (For extra fun, try to add another sentence to complete the sequence!)

1. Roll out the cookie dough.
   Cut out cookies with a cookie cutter.

   _____.

2. Put your dog into the soapy water.
   Fill a tub with water and soap.

   _____.

3. Add water to the dog food.
   Put dog food in a bowl.

   _____.

4. Pack your suitcase.
   Drive to the airport.

   _____.

5. Paint your fence.
   Buy paint and paintbrushes.

   _____.

6. Take your bike out of the garage.
   Go for a bike ride.

   _____.

_____   _____   _____   Game Board 1
          Name   Homework Partner   Date   **Let's Give Information**

     #BK-308 Positive Pragmatic Game Boards Fun Sheets • ©2003 Super Duper® Publications • 1-800-277-8737 • Online! www.superduperinc.com

Spin a Sequence

Instructions: If you prefer, glue this page to construction paper for added durability. Cut out the arrow/dial. Use a brad to connect the dial to the circle. Spin the spinner. Give three or more sentences to tell how to complete the sequence. _____

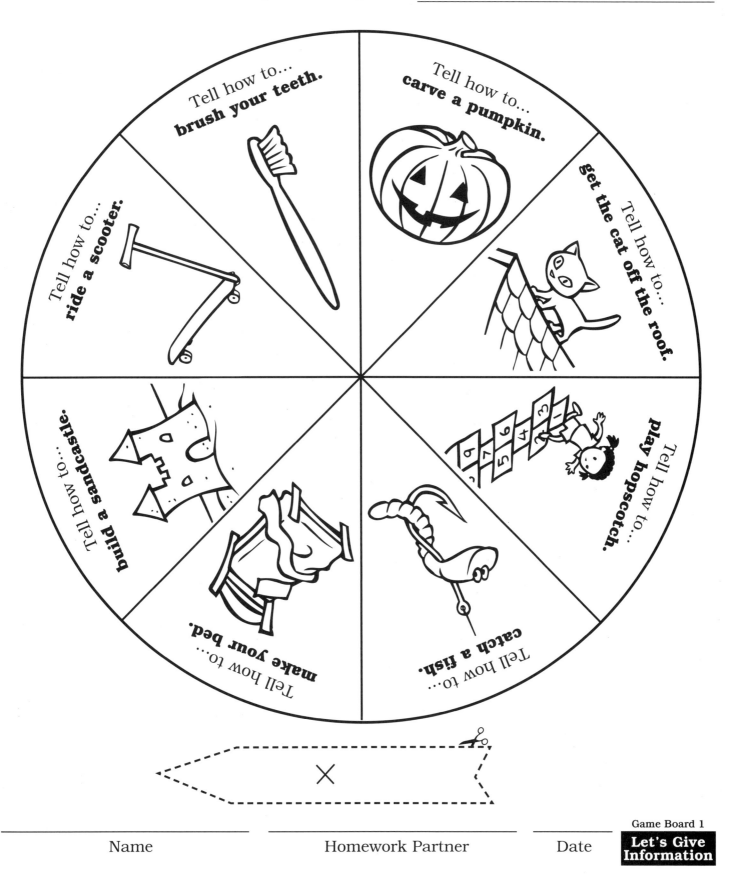

_____   _____   _____

Find the Star

Instructions: If you prefer, glue this page to construction paper for added durability. Cut out all the cards and place them face up on the table. Cut out the star. Player One hides the star under one of the pictures. Player Two chooses a picture, gives three steps to describe that sequence, then checks to see if the star is hidden under that picture. Take turns hiding the star and saying the sequence of steps until all the cards have been used.

Tell how to wash a car.	Tell how to make a sundae.	Tell how to ride a bike.
Tell how to make popcorn.	Tell how to wash a dog.	Tell how to make a sandwich.
Tell how to wrap a present.	Tell how to paint a fence.	Tell how to decorate a Christmas tree.

_____   _____   _____
          Name   Homework Partner   Date

Game Board 1

Let's Give Information

Picnic in the Park

Instructions: Look at each picture. Finish each sentence with three different activities needed to complete that part of the sequence. (For example, to get ready, you must pack a lunch. What else?) _____

To get ready for a picnic, you must...

1. _____

2. _____

3. _____

While you're there, you can...

1. _____

2. _____

3. _____

When it's time to go, you should...

1. _____

2. _____

3. _____

_____   _____   _____   Game Board 1

Name   Homework Partner   Date

Let's Give Information

Sequencing Race

Instructions: Cut out the game markers below. Flip a coin. Heads moves one space. Tails moves two spaces. Choose your racetrack. Take turns flipping the coin and racing down the track. As you land on a space, tell at least three steps needed to complete that sequence.

Tell how to...

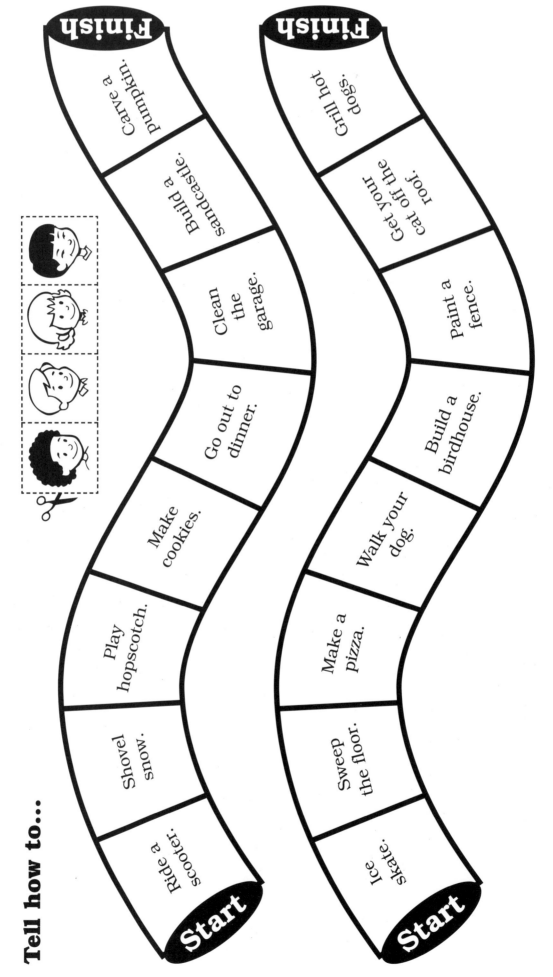

Track 1 (Start to Finish): Ride a scooter. / Shovel snow. / Play hopscotch. / Make cookies. / Go out to dinner. / Clean the garage. / Build a sandcastle. / Carve a pumpkin.

Track 2 (Start to Finish): Ice skate. / Sweep the floor. / Make a pizza. / Walk your dog. / Build a birdhouse. / Paint a fence. / Get your cat off the roof. / Grill hot dogs.

Name _____ Homework Partner _____ Date _____

Sequencing Charades

Instructions: If you prefer, glue this page to construction paper for added durability. Cut out the cards and place them face down on the table. Player One picks up a card and acts out the sequence. Player Two describes the actions and guesses the sequence acted out by Player One. Take turns!

How to... plant a flower.

How to... ride a scooter.

How to... walk your dog.

How to... make lemonade.

How to... build a snowman.

How to... catch a fish.

How to... shampoo your hair.

How to... brush your teeth.

How to... go ice skating.

How to... make cookies.

How to... wash dishes.

How to... play hopscotch.

Super Duper Pizza Shop

Instructions: Find these three events in the picture below: a man making pizza, a man washing dishes, customers entering the shop for dinner. Describe each event using at least three steps for each one.

Name _____   Homework Partner _____   Date _____

Game Board 2

"Talk Me Into It!"

Persuasion Skills

Choosing Good Reasons

Instructions: Read/listen to each statement below. Then put a check (✔) in each picture box that shows a good reason for the statement.

1. What are good reasons for Mom to buy you new shoes?

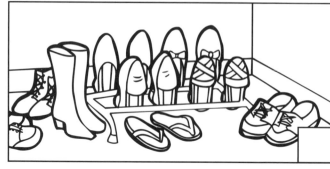

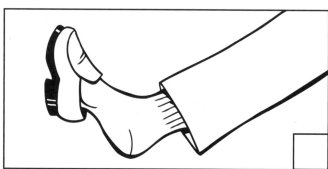

2. What are good reasons for Dad to play basketball with you?

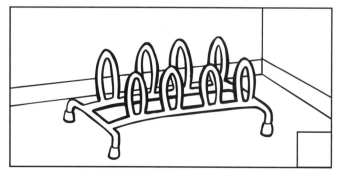

It's great to spend some time together.

Let me show you some things, son.

I'm exhausted right now.

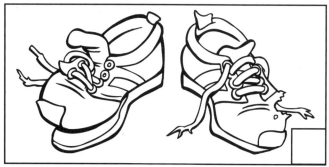

_____ _____ _____ **Game Board 2**

Name   Homework Partner   Date   **"Talk Me Into It!"**

What's the Best Way to Persuade?

Instructions: Read each sentence. Look at the pictures and each way the person tries to persuade someone. Put a check (✔) in the picture that shows the best way to persuade.

1. You want your sister to help you clean up the bedroom.

2. You want your brother to take your turn feeding the dog.

3. You want your mom to take you to the beach.

#BK-308 Positive Pragmatic Game Boards Fun Sheets • ©2003 Super Duper® Publications • 1-800-277-8737 • Online! www.superduperinc.com

Say a Reason

Instructions: Listen to your Helper read each request. Complete each request by giving a good reason. _____

1. Mom, could you please let me get ice cream because _____

    _____?

2. Dad, would you play catch with me because _____

    _____?

3. Joey, will you fix my bike because _____

    _____?

4. Mrs. Jones, can you give us a night off from homework because _____

    _____?

5. Mary, can I borrow your pink sweater because _____

    _____?

6. Grandma, will you bake chocolate chip cookies because _____

    _____?

7. Sue, can I have some of your popcorn because _____

    _____?

8. Mom, can Mary stay over for dinner because _____

    _____?

Game Board 2

| Name | Homework Partner | Date | "Talk Me Into It!" |

#BK-308 Positive Pragmatic Game Boards Fun Sheets • ©2003 Super Duper® Publications • 1-800-277-8737 • Online! www.superduperinc.com

Is This a Good Reason?

Instructions: Read each question. If the picture shows a good reason, color it. If the picture does not show a good reason, put an X on it. _____

Is this a good reason to...

1. get new shoes?

2. have no homework?

3. get a pet?

4. get pizza for dinner?

5. get a new bike?

Good Reason - Bad Reason

Instructions: Read/listen to each sentence. If the sentence gives a good reason, color the happy face. If the reason is not good, color the sad face. Bonus: Provide a better reason.

1. Mom, take me shopping now! I want to go!

2. Sis, if you help me clean my room, I'll help you with yours.

3. Dad, if you play ball with me, I'll help you with the yard work.

4. Mrs. Green, if you postpone the test, we'll all have two more nights to study. I'm sure we'll all pass.

5. Mom, please buy me a cat. Deb has a cat and I want one too!

6. Dad, can I have ice cream from the ice cream man? I really love ice cream.

7. John, will you take out the garbage for me? I'll walk the dog for you.

8. Mr. Jones, can we have a school dance? I will make sure there are plenty of adults to watch us.

_____ _____ _____
Name   Homework Partner   Date

Game Board 2

"Talk Me Into It!"

#BK-308 Positive Pragmatic Game Boards Fun Sheets • ©2003 Super Duper® Publications • 1-800-277-8737 • Online! www.superduperinc.com

Please Buy Me a Puppy!

Instructions: Read the story below. Fill in the blanks with words that will persuade Mom to buy you the puppy. _____

"Mom," said Bobby, "I would really like a new puppy because _____

_____ .

"Bobby, a puppy is a lot of work and a big responsibility," said Mom.

"Besides, Dad and I will probably get stuck doing all the work!"

"Mom, I promise I'll _____ ,

_____ , and _____

_____ ," said Bobby.

"Mom, you won't have to do one thing," begged Bobby.

"Okay," said Mom. "You talked me into it. Now let's see if we can

persuade your dad!"

_____   _____   _____   **Game Board 2**

Name   Homework Partner   Date

#BK-308 Positive Pragmatic Game Boards Fun Sheets • ©2003 Super Duper® Publications • 1-800-277-8737 • Online! www.superduperinc.com

Give Three Reasons

Instructions: Look at the picture below. Write or say three reasons to persuade your mother to let you have a friend sleep over. _____

1. _____

_____

2. _____

_____

3. _____

_____

Give a Reason Why

Instructions: Read each sentence below. Give reason(s) for each picture.

PET SHOP

Why should Mom buy
you a pet?

_____

_____

_____

_____

CLUBHOUSE

Why should Dad build
you a clubhouse?

_____

_____

_____

_____

Why should Mom take
you to the park?

_____

_____

_____

_____

Why should your brother
help you clean the garage?

_____

_____

_____

Name	Homework Partner	Date	Game Board 2
			"Talk Me Into It!"

What Could You Do in Return?

Instructions: Listen as your helper reads each question. Tell what you could do in return.

1. What could you do for Mom if she takes you shopping?

2. What could you do for Dad if he plays baseball with you?

3. What could you do for your brother if he fixes your bike?

4. What could you do for Grandma if she bakes you cookies?

5. What could you do for your sister if she lets you borrow her new toy?

6. What could you do for your teacher if he gives no homework?

7. What could you do for your friend if he helps you with a science project?

8. What could you do for your neighbor if he lets you swim in his pool?

9. What could you do for the principal if he lets you have a "sports day" at school?

10. What could you do for your mom if she buys you a puppy?

11. What could you do for your dad if he builds you a tree house?

12. What could you do for your friend if he goes to the park with you?

Game Board 2

_____ _____ _____
Name   Homework Partner   Date

"Talk Me Into It!"

#BK-308 Positive Pragmatic Game Boards Fun Sheets • ©2003 Super Duper® Publications • 1-800-277-8737 • Online! www.superduperinc.com

Talk Me Into It!

Instructions: Look at the pictures below. Read the words that are written in each bubble. Fill in the empty bubbles with words that will persuade your mom to take you to the mall.

Mom, will you please take me to the mall?

I'm sorry but I have too much to do around the house.

Okay, let's go! You talked me into it.

Thanks, Mom!

_____   _____   _____
Name   Homework Partner   Date

Game Board 2

"Talk Me Into It!"

#BK-308 Positive Pragmatic Game Boards Fun Sheets • ©2003 Super Duper® Publications • 1-800-277-8737 • Online! www.superduperinc.com

Act It Out

Instructions: If you prefer, glue this page to construction paper for added durability. Cut out the cards and place them face down in a pile on the table. Have the student choose a card and a partner. The student will then try to persuade his/her partner to do what is written on the card. Take turns.

✂

Persuade your partner...  to play basketball with you.	Persuade your partner...  to buy you ice cream.	Persuade your partner...  to bake chocolate chip cookies.
Persuade your partner...  to loan you his walkman.	Persuade your partner...  to drive you and your friends to the beach.	Persuade your partner...  to let you have a hamster.
Persuade your partner... 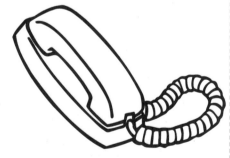 to let you have a telephone in your room.	Persuade your partner...  to buy you new sneakers.	Persuade your partner...  to help shovel snow.

_____   _____   _____   Game Board 2

Name   Homework Partner   Date

"Talk Me Into It!"

    #BK-308 Positive Pragmatic Game Boards Fun Sheets • ©2003 Super Duper® Publications • 1-800-277-8737 • Online! www.superduperinc.com

Tic-Tac-Toe

Instructions: Cut out the Tic-Tac-Toe markers below. One player gets "X's" and the other gets "O's". Player One covers a picture and provides a persuasion for the given situation. Player Two follows in turn. Three in a row wins! _____

Persuade Mom to buy you a jacket. 	Persuade Dad to take you to the new skate park. 	Persuade your brother to rake the leaves with you. 
Persuade your friend to join the hockey team. 	Persuade your sister to clean your room. 	Persuade your teacher to have a "Food From Around the World" day. 
Persuade your parents to take you on a camping trip. 	Persuade your neighbor to let you play football in his backyard. 	Persuade your babysitter to let you stay up late. 

_____   _____   _____   Game Board 2

Name   Homework Partner   Date   **"Talk Me Into It!"**

The Answer is "No"

Instructions: Read each sentence. Fill in each blank with a reason why the answer might be "No."

1. I asked Mom to buy pizza for dinner. She said, "No" because _____
_____.

2. I asked my teacher to postpone the test. She said, "No" because _____
_____.

3. I asked Dad to build a clubhouse for me. He said, "No" because _____
_____.

4. I asked my friend to join the baseball team. He said, "No" because _____
_____.

5. I asked Mom if my friend could sleep over. She said, "No" because _____
_____.

6. I asked the principal if we could have a "Bring Your Pet to School" day.
He said, "No" because _____
_____.

7. I asked my sister to help me clean the house. She said, "No" because
_____.

8. I asked my babysitter if we could go to the park. She said, "No" because
_____.

9. I asked my friend if he could walk my dog after school. He said, "No" because
_____.

10. I asked my mom if she could buy me new sneakers. She said, "No" because
_____.

_____   _____   _____

Name   Homework Partner   Date

Game Board 2

"Talk Me Into It!"

A New Cereal

Instructions: Look at the cereal box below. Try to talk your mom into buying this new cereal. Look on the cereal box for good reasons. _____

#BK-308 Positive Pragmatic Game Boards Fun Sheets • ©2003 Super Duper® Publications • 1-800-277-8737 • Online! www.superduperinc.com

31

A New Product

Instructions: Create your own product. You might want to invent an amazing new chewing gum, a homework robot, or a cereal that makes you super smart! Draw a picture of your product in the box below. Persuade people to buy your product. You must give people good reasons to buy it. Have fun! _____

Buy _____. It _____
(name of product)

_____
(Give reasons people should buy your product.)

_____

_____

_____

_____   _____   _____   Game Board 2
Name   Homework Partner   Date

"Talk Me Into It!"

#BK-308 Positive Pragmatic Game Boards Fun Sheets • ©2003 Super Duper® Publications • 1-800-277-8737 • Online! www.superduperinc.com

Game Board 3

What Would You Ask?

Requesting

Ask a Good Question

Instructions: Read/listen to each situation and the following two questions. Which question should you ask? Draw a happy face in the circle next to the good question. Draw a sad face next to the one that does not make sense.

1. Your Mom says, "I have to go on a trip!"

    Where are you going, Mom? ◯

    When do we eat, Mom? ◯

2. Your teacher says, "We will have a test!"

    Do we have gym today? ◯

    When is the test? ◯

3. Your Dad says, "Please go to the store for me!"

    What do you need at the store? ◯

    May I go to the playground now? ◯

4. Your principal says, "I need some help after school."

    When is our next vacation? ◯

    What can I do to help you? ◯

5. Your friend says, "I have to leave school early."

    Why do you have to leave early? ◯

    What did you bring for lunch? ◯

6. Your brother says, "I need a Band-Aid® quickly!"

    What happened to you? ◯

    Can I borrow your bike? ◯

Name   Homework Partner   Date

    #BK-308 Positive Pragmatic Game Boards Fun Sheets • ©2003 Super Duper® Publications • 1-800-277-8737 • Online! www.superduperinc.com

Picture-Question Match

Instructions: Look at each picture on the left. Draw a line to match each picture with the correct question on the right.

Do you want your bottle now?

Excuse me, can you please tell me where to find the bathroom?

Where did you buy those new toys?

What art supplies do we need?

Why is there a puddle of water on the floor?

Choose the Question

Instructions: Cut out the "question boxes" at the bottom of this page. Glue each question box in the correct blank box in the pictures.

When will the new jungle gym be ready?

Where will the club meet?

May I borrow your skateboard?

How much food should I give the dog?

What is so funny, girls?

What time is the open house?

_____   _____   _____
Name   Homework Partner   Date

Game Board 3

What Would You Ask?

#BK-308 Positive Pragmatic Game Boards Fun Sheets • ©2003 Super Duper® Publications • 1-800-277-8737 • Online! www.superduperinc.com

Ask and Find Out

Instructions: Look at each picture below. What do you need to find out about each situation? Complete each "wh" question. Ask your question aloud.

Someone is having a party. What do you need to ask?

Who _____

_____?

What _____

_____?

When _____

_____?

Where _____

_____?

Your friend wants you to go to a movie. What do you need to ask?

Who _____

_____?

What _____

_____?

When _____

_____?

Where _____

_____?

_____   _____   _____

Name   Homework Partner   Date

Game Board 3

What Would You Ask?

Help!

Instructions: Your friend has lost his dog! Try to help him find the dog by asking him good questions. Use the word box at the bottom of the page. _____

1. _____ ?

2. _____ ?

3. _____ ?

4. _____ ?

5. _____ ?

These words may help you start your questions. You may use the words more than once, or use your own starter words.

What	Where	When	Who

_____   _____   _____

Name   Homework Partner   Date

Game Board 3

What Would You Ask?

38   #BK-308 Positive Pragmatic Game Boards Fun Sheets • ©2003 Super Duper® Publications • 1-800-277-8737 • Online! www.superduperinc.com

Ask a Question Tic-Tac-Toe

Instructions: Cut out the Tic-Tac-Toe tokens below. One player gets "X's" and the other gets "O's." Player One chooses a square, reads or listens to what is happening in the picture, and asks a question. Player Two follows in turn. Three in a row wins!

 Dad is taking your family on vacation.	 You see your friends playing a new game.	 Your baby sister is crying.
 Your teacher says, "We have an assembly today."	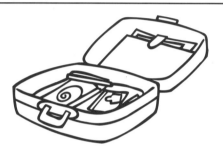 Your friend just got home from his vacation.	 Your brother wants to borrow your bike.
 Someone found a book that might be yours.	 Grandma needs your help.	 Mom says, "We are going out to celebrate."

_____   _____   _____
Name   Homework Partner   Date

What Would You Ask?

Snack Time

Instructions: Read/listen to the story below. Complete each blank with a question sentence. Ask each question aloud. (Each question has been started for you! You may want to read the whole story first to help you ask the correct questions.)

"Bobby," Miss Jones said, "Don't forget! Tomorrow, it is your turn to bring in a snack for our class!" Bobby asked, "What _____

_____?" Miss Jones answered, "You can bring in any healthy snack." Bobby decided to bring in banana muffins! He asked, "How many _____?" Miss Jones said, "We have 20 children in our class, Bobby, so..." Bobby said, "Okay, I will bring in 20 banana muffins...oops and one for you, Miss Jones! That makes 21 banana muffins! I'll remind my mom! When _____

_____?" Miss Jones answered, "Snack time is at 11:00 a.m." Finally, Bobby asked, "Where _____

_____?" Miss Jones replied, "Tell your Mom to bring the muffins to Room 101." Miss Jones and her class cannot wait until snack time tomorrow for those yummy (and healthy!) banana muffins!

Act It Out

Instructions: If you prefer, glue this page to construction paper for added durability. Cut out the cards and place them face down on the table. Player One chooses a card and asks a question about the situation on the card. Player Two answers the question. Take turns asking and answering. Act out each situation. _____

Grandpa can't find his reading glasses.

Jack fell off his bike.

Your sister wants to borrow your sweater.

The baby is sad.

Your friend wants to go to the park.

Dad wants to go camping.

It is your turn to bring a class snack.

You see your friends shooting basketball hoops.

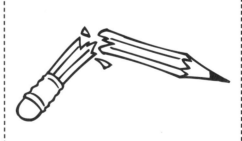

You broke your last pencil.

_____   _____   _____   Game Board 3

Name   Homework Partner   Date

What Would You Ask?

Spinner Fun

Instructions: If you prefer, glue this page to construction paper for added durability. Cut out the arrow/dial. Use a brad to connect the dial to the circle. Spin the spinner. Look at the picture and read the sentence. Choose a question word from around the outside of the spinner. Ask a question about each picture using a question word.

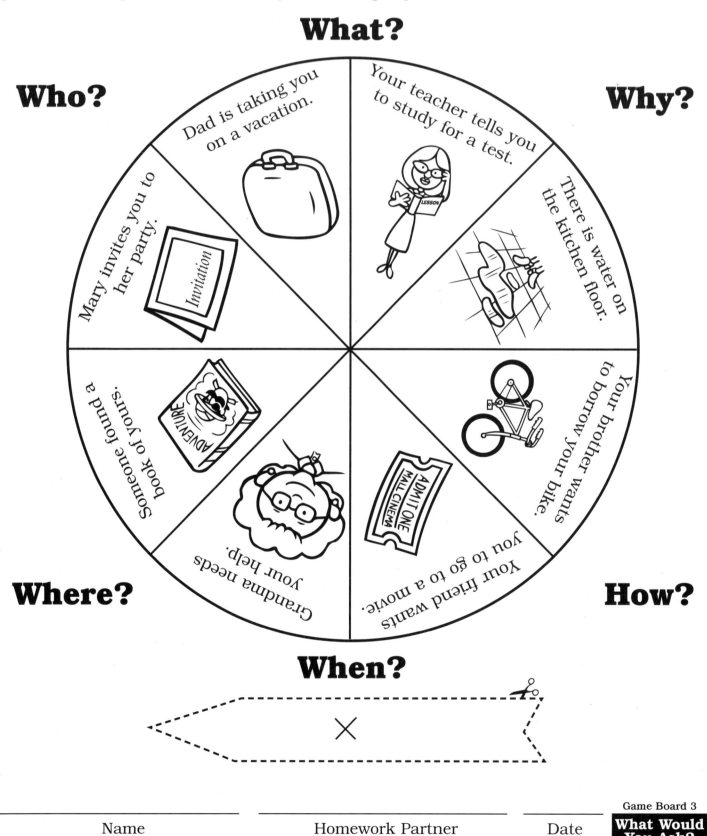

#BK-308 Positive Pragmatic Game Boards Fun Sheets • ©2003 Super Duper® Publications • 1-800-277-8737 • Online! www.superduperinc.com

Game Board 3

What Would You Ask?

Name _____ Homework Partner _____ Date _____

Mystery Animals

Instructions: If you prefer, glue the bottom half of this page to construction paper for added durability. Cut out the cards and place them face down on the table. Player One chooses a card (the mystery animal!) Other players try to guess the mystery animal by asking questions. Take turns!

Here are some examples of questions to get started:

1. Where does it (live, sleep, etc.) ?

2. What does it (eat, say, do, etc.) ?

3. Does it have (wings, horns, etc.) ?

4. How many (legs does it have, etc.) ?

5. How does (it move, find food, etc.) ?

_____   _____   _____   Game Board 3

Name   Homework Partner   Date   **What Would You Ask?**

Ask the Right Questions

Instructions: Look at each picture below. Cut on the dotted line above each picture to make a slot. Cut out the question strips at the bottom of the page. Read each question and place it in the correct slot!

There is a new after-school club.

Someone found a book you think might be yours.

Your friend has to leave school early.

(After you place the question strips in the slots, try to think of another question for each picture!)

| Does it have a red cover? | Where are you going? | Who is the author? |
| Are you coming back a little later? | When does it start? | Where does it meet? |

Name

Homework Partner

Date

Do – Does – Did

Instructions: Read/listen to each sentence below. Ask a question about each situation. Start each question with Do, Does, or Did. _____

1. You need to know if your brother went to baseball practice. You would ask your mom:

_____ ?

2. You need to know if your teacher needs help after school. You would ask your teacher:

_____ ?

3. You need to know if Rover needs to be walked. You would ask your dad:

_____ ?

4. You need to know if your friend wants to go to a movie. You would ask your friend:

_____ ?

5. You need to know if your mom remembered to sign your homework. You would ask your mom:

_____ ?

6. You need to know if a brontosaurus ate meat. You would ask your teacher:

_____ ?

7. You need to know if an elephant lives in a forest or a jungle. You would ask your older brother:

_____ ?

8. You need to know if your friend has an extra pencil. You would ask your friend:

_____ ?

_____ _____ _____

Name   Homework Partner   Date

Game Board 3

What Would You Ask?

Question or Statement

Instructions: Look at each picture below. Next to each picture is a question and a statement. Decide which one is a question and add a question mark. Decide which one is a statement and add a period. (Bonus: Change each statement into a question.)

1. Mom ran out of bread.

   What do you need at the store____

   Mom needs more bread____

2. There is a science fair at school.

   I finally finished my science project____

   Who will judge the science project____

3. Your friend gets a new toy.

   I need one of those____

   How much did that cost____

4. The principal asks you to help him after school.

   How can I help you____

   I'll see you after school____

5. Your friend just got back from vacation.

   I missed you____

   Where did you go____

6. You are going on a class trip.

   Do you want to sit together on the bus____

   Class trips are fun____

Game Board 3

What Would You Ask?

Name   Homework Partner   Date

#BK-308 Positive Pragmatic Game Boards Fun Sheets • ©2003 Super Duper® Publications • 1-800-277-8737 • Online! www.superduperinc.com

Answering Questions

Instructions: Look at each picture below. Read/listen to the statement next to each picture. Put a check (✔) next to the correct question for each statement.

	We eat at noon. ❏ Where do we eat lunch? ❏ What are we having for lunch? ❏ When do we eat lunch?
	Your sister borrowed your sweater. ❏ Who has my new sweater? ❏ When can I wear my new sweater? ❏ What color is the new sweater?
	Work was busy today. ❏ How did you get to work? ❏ When do you go to work? ❏ How was work today?
	We can make apple pie. ❏ Where is dinner? ❏ What can we make for dessert? ❏ Who is making dinner?
	I hurt my knee. ❏ Why are you crying? ❏ Where is your bike? ❏ When do you ride your bike?
	I am going to the golf course. ❏ What is your favorite sport? ❏ Where are you going? ❏ How are you getting to the golf course?

Game Board 3

What Would You Ask?

_____ _____ _____

Name   Homework Partner   Date

Conversation Time

Instructions: Mom and Dad are taking a trip. What would the children ask Mom? Ask the question that belongs in each empty conversation bubble. (Read/listen to Mom's answers so you know what questions the kids asked her!)

Game Board 4

It's Telephone Time

Telephone Etiquette

Who Would You Call?

Instructions: Draw a line to connect each situation to the person you should call.

Who would you call if...

1. ... you saw smoke?

operator

2. ... someone broke into your home?

fireman

3. ... you have a toothache?

pizza chef

4. ... you need a friend's number?

dentist

5. ... you're hungry and there is nothing to eat?

police (911)

6. ... your grandma doesn't feel well?

doctor

Name   Homework Partner   Date

Game Board 4

It's Telephone Time

Is This Appropriate Phone Use?

Instructions: Read the comment in each bubble. Color the happy face if the comment shows appropriate phone use. Color the sad face if the comment is not appropriate.

Name   Homework Partner   Date

What Should I Say?

Instructions: Use the reference chart below to help you in these three telephone conversations. Your partner will start each conversation. Go back and forth until the conversation ends. Then go to the next conversation.

Hold on, please.	Who's calling, please?	What's your number?
She/He can't come to the phone right now.	May I take a message?	I'll give Mom the message.
I'll tell Mom you called.	Thank you for calling.	Goodbye!

1. Hello, this is Dr. Brown's office. May I please speak to your Mom?

2. Hi, may I speak to your dad?

3. Hi, this is Tom. May I speak to your brother?

Let's Call For a Pizza

Instructions: Fill in the bubbles with information to complete each conversation.

911 Emergency

Instructions: There is an emergency in your home and you need help. It is important to give the emergency operator information so he/she can help you. Follow the guidelines below. Remember to always stay calm and speak slowly and clearly.

1.   Tell the operator what you need.

   I need an ambulance, police, fire department, etc.

   _____

2.   Tell the operator your address:

   I live at...

   _____

3.   Tell the operator your name.

   My name is...

   _____

4.   Give the operator any other important information.

   _____

   _____

Bonus: Let's pretend you see smoke coming from your neighbor's house. Have your partner pretend to be the emergency operator. Call 911 and ask for help.

_____   _____   _____
      Name   Homework Partner   Date

Game Board 4

It's Telephone Time

   #BK-308 Positive Pragmatic Game Boards Fun Sheets • ©2003 Super Duper® Publications • 1-800-277-8737 • Online! www.superduperinc.com

Let's Take a Message

Instructions: Read/listen to the message from Dr. Jones' office. Fill in the information on the message pad at the bottom of the page. _____

This is Dr. Jones' office calling. Jimmy Smith has an appointment at 2:00 p.m. tomorrow. Please have your mom, Mrs. Smith, call back at 555-7245.

Message Pad

Who called?_____

Who is the message for?_____

What is the message?_____

_____

What is the caller's phone number?_____

When did the person call? (Date and time.)

_____

_____ _____ _____

Name   Homework Partner   Date

Game Board 4

It's Telephone Time

Telephone Time Spinner

Instructions: If you prefer, glue this page to construction paper for added durability. Cut out the arrow/dial. Use a brad to connect the dial to the circle. Spin the spinner. Pretend you are talking on the telephone. Tell what you would say. Choose a conversation partner to answer you. _____

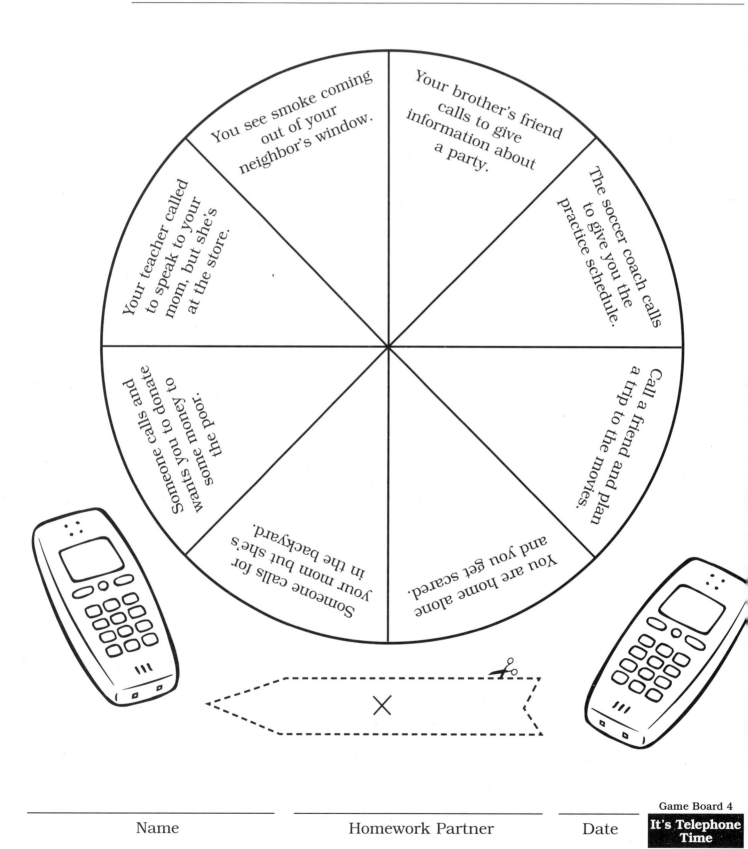

You see smoke coming out of your neighbor's window.

Your brother's friend calls to give information about a party.

Your teacher called to speak to your mom, but she's at the store.

The soccer coach calls to give you the practice schedule.

Someone calls and wants you to donate some money to the poor.

Call a friend and plan a trip to the movies.

Someone calls for your mom but she's in the backyard.

You are home alone and you get scared.

Let's Talk

Instructions: If you prefer, glue this page to construction paper for added durability. Cut out the cards and place them face down on the table. Take turns choosing a card. Have the telephone conversation indicated on the card with a partner.

You forgot your trumpet. Call Mom and ask her if she can bring it to school.	Your forgot your spelling homework. Call a friend and ask for the words.	Call the dentist's office to cancel your appointment. Don't forget to reschedule it!	You want to invite your friend to your house for dinner.
Your brother needs a ride home from football practice but Mom is not home.	Call and order Chinese food.	Call 911. There was a car accident in front of your home.	The gas station calls to tell Dad his car is ready.
A friend calls to see if you can sleep over.	Call your grandma to see how she's feeling.	Call information to get your friend's phone number. (You have to know his/her last name and address.)	Someone calls to speak to Dad, but only Mom is home.
You call your friend but dialed the wrong number.	A magazine salesman calls but your parents are not home.	You need to call your mom at work to tell her you will be staying after school. Her secretary answers the phone.	Your grandpa fell and you need an ambulance.

_____   _____   _____

Name   Homework Partner   Date

Game Board 4

It's Telephone Time

Find It in the Yellow Pages

Instructions: The *Yellow Pages* is a telephone book that gives the phone numbers of different businesses. Cut out the *Yellow Pages* on pages 58 and 59. Place the pages with letters in alphabetical order. Attach the *Yellow Pages* cover on top and staple to make your own telephone book. Then, try to find the information you need on the "Find It" page.

Restaurants

Apple Annie's American Diner 555-1110

Bezzini's Italian Food 555-0005

Chow's China Garden 555-0101

Deli Delights 555-1775

Eastern Thai.........................555-4570

Southern Spice Shack 555-4523

Doctors (Physicians)

Dr. Eppie Dermis
Skin Care Specialist 555-2300

Dr. Steven Kidd
Pediatrician 555-6789
We Specialize in Children!

Dr. Mi Shu
Podiatrist....................1-800-555-FOOT
The Foot Place

Brown's Brake Barn 555-5762

Casey's Used Cars......................555-1392

Dennis' Oil Changing 555-0010

Fix-em-up Body Shop 555-1110

Tune-up Time 555-5010

World Tires 555-6167

Community Information

Court House 555-1462

Fire Department 555-3110

Police Department 555-5000

Public Library 555-7777

Public School District 555-1221

_____ _____ _____
Name   Homework Partner   Date

Game Board 4

It's Telephone Time

Find It in the Yellow Pages

Instructions: Cut out the pages below along the dotted lines. Follow the directions on page 58.

Movers

 *We Move Anything Anywhere!*

Movers........................ 555-MOVE

Movers 555-1273

We Haul ....555-4444

Pools

Brand New Pools...................1-555-POOLS

Don's Pool Cleaning 555-7070

Pete's Pool Installers....................555-9101

Swim Right Pool Supplies 555-2232

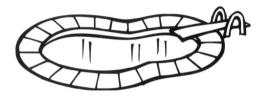

Yellow Pages

staple

staple

Find It!!!

1. You would like to go out for dinner. Find a place to eat. Write down the name and phone number.

_____

2. You need a book for a book report. You want to see if the library has it. Find the library phone number. _____

3. You have a rash. Who would you call?

_____

4. You need a set of tires for your car. Who would you call? _____

5. You need someone to clean your swimming pool. Who would you call?

_____

_____   _____   _____

Name   Homework Partner   Date

Game Board 4

It's Telephone Time

Place an Order

Instructions: Take a look at this page from Super Duper's Clothing (SDC) Catalog. Call SDC and place an order. Have your homework helper be the SDC operator. You can use the order form below to organize your information before you call.

Super Swimwear

$49.99

Item # 1X4C
Sizes: S-M-L
Colors: Red, Blue, Yellow

Super Long Sleeved Shirt

$29.99

Item # 456B
Sizes: S-M-L-XL
Colors: Blue, White, Pink

Denim Super Slacks

$39.99

Item # 789C
Sizes: 4, 6, 8, 10, 12, 14
Colors: Blue, Black

Leather Shoes

$29.99

Item # 1015
Sizes: 5, 5½, 6, 6½, 7, 7½, 8, 8½, 9, 9½
Colors: Brown, Black, Gray, Navy

Super Sun Hat

$19.99

Item # 206 F
Sizes: S-M-L
Colors: White, Black, Red

Super Skirt

$25.99

Item # 305HZ
Sizes: 4-14
Colors: Green, Gray, Yellow, Blue

CALL 1-800-87SUPER TO PLACE AN ORDER

Item #	Name	Color	Size	Price
			Total	

_____   _____   _____

Name   Homework Partner   Date

#BK-308 Positive Pragmatic Game Boards Fun Sheets • ©2003 Super Duper® Publications • 1-800-277-8737 • Online! www.superduperinc.com

What's the Number?

Instructions: You want to call your friend who moved away. You must call 411 (Information) to get your friend's phone number. You must be able to give the operator some important information so he can help you. Fill in the information in the box below.

_____   _____
What is your friend's last name?   What is your friend's father's first name?

_____   _____
What is the city your friend lives in?   What is the state your friend lives in?

Now that you have all the information you need, you may call the 411 operator. Your Homework Partner will be the operator. You will answer his/her questions using the information above. Don't forget to have a piece of paper and a pencil ready to write down the number.

Operator: *Hello, this is the operator. May I help you?*

Caller: (Tell the operator what you need.)

Operator: *Can you spell the last name?* (Caller replies.)

Operator: *What city and state?* (Caller replies.)

Operator: *What is your friend's father's name?* (Caller replies.)

Operator: *The number is _____.*

_____   _____   _____   Game Board 4
Name   Homework Partner   Date   **It's Telephone Time**

Let's Leave a Message

Instructions: You call your friend to get the spelling words. No one is home, so you must leave a message on the answering machine. Don't forget to give your name, phone number, and a short message.

Hello, we can't come to the phone right now. Please leave your name, number, and a brief message when you hear the beep.

Write or say your message:

Important Phone Numbers

Instructions: If you prefer, glue this sheet to construction paper for added durability. Fill in the blanks with phone numbers you might need in an emergency. Cut out the page along the dotted lines. Use a hole puncher to make a hole where indicated. Put a piece of yarn through the hole. Tie the two ends of the yarn together so you can hang your phone list near the telephone for quick reference. _____

Important Phone Numbers

Mom at work: _____

Dad at work: _____

Doctor: _____

Fire Dept: _____

Police: _____

Neighbor: Mr/Mrs. _____
Name

_____

School: _____

Other: _____

_____

Telephone Manners

Instructions: How would you respond to each situation? Use your telephone manners.

What would you say if . . .

1. Mom is on the phone and you need to make a call?

   _____

2. Someone called for Mom and she's not home?

   _____

3. You want to end a conversation?

   _____

4. Your dad gets a call and he's in the shower?

   _____

5. You need to get paper and a pencil to take a message?

   _____

6. You are taking a message and you can't spell the caller's name?

   _____

7. A stranger calls and starts asking you for personal information?

   _____

8. You are talking and your mom needs to make a phone call?

   _____

_____   _____   _____

Name   Homework Partner   Date

Game Board 4

It's Telephone Time

#BK-308 Positive Pragmatic Game Boards Fun Sheets • ©2003 Super Duper® Publications • 1-800-277-8737 • Online! www.superduperinc.com

Game Board 5

What Should You Do?

Problem Solving

Problem Solving Puzzle

Instructions: Cut out the puzzle pieces on page 67. Pick a puzzle piece and read the problem. Find the piece on this page that tells the solution. Place the problem piece on the solution piece.

Give your brother one of your toys.

Tell the security guard that you are lost.

Call 911.

Introduce yourself.

Wipe up the milk.

Take the ring to "Lost and Found."

Tell Mom you are sorry.

Get a stepstool.

Call your friend to get the spelling words.

Break the cookie in half.

Ask the librarian for help.

Offer to pay for the broken window.

Name

Homework Partner

Date

Game Board 5

What Should You Do?

#BK-308 Positive Pragmatic Game Boards Fun Sheets • ©2003 Super Duper® Publications • 1-800-277-8737 • Online! www.superduperinc.com

Problem Solving Puzzle

Instructions: Cut out the puzzle pieces below. Follow the instructions on page 66.

Your little brother keeps taking your toys.

You get lost at the mall.

You see smoke coming from a neighbor's home.

There is a new kid in your class. He doesn't know anyone.

You spilled milk on your homework paper.

You found a gold ring on the playground.

You broke your Mom's best vase.

You want a snack but you can't reach the cookie jar.

You have a spelling test tomorrow and you left your spelling book at school.

You and your brother both want a cookie but there is only one left.

You cannot find the book you need at the local library.

You broke your neighbor's window with a baseball.

Name

Homework Partner

Date

Color the Best Solution

Instructions: Look at each problem picture on the left. Read/describe the problem. Next, look at the following two pictures on the right. Talk about the pictures. Color or circle the one that shows the better solution.

A girl on your bus always teases you.

Make a face at her.

Ignore her.

You lost your house key.

Go next door and ask your neighbor for help.

Sit on the stoop and cry.

You have to do a project and you run out of glue.

Get angry.

Ask your friend to share his glue with you.

Game Board 5

What Should You Do?

_____ Name _____ Homework Partner _____ Date

#BK-308 Positive Pragmatic Game Boards Fun Sheets • ©2003 Super Duper® Publications • 1-800-277-8737 • Online! www.superduperinc.com

Correct Solution? Yes or No

Instructions: Listen to your helper read each item below. If you hear a correct solution color "Yes." If you hear an incorrect solution color "No." Bonus: For the incorrect solutions tell what you could do instead.

1. There is a run away dog near your house.

   You should pet it.

2. You took your friend's jacket home by mistake.

   You should call your friend to tell her you have her jacket.

3. A strange car is following you as you walk home.

   You should ask the driver what he wants.

4. Some kids start a club, but they say you can't join.

   You should ask some other kids to start a club.

5. You miss the school bus in the morning.

   You should just stay home and play.

6. One of your friends is calling you names.

   You should tell her to please stop.

7. Your loose tooth falls out while you are eating lunch.

   You should ask to go see the nurse.

8. You left your lunch at home.

   You should take your friend's lunch.

Game Board 5

What Should You Do?

_____   _____   _____
Name   Homework Partner   Date

Cut and Paste a Solution

Instructions: Cut out the solution pictures at the bottom of the page. Read/listen to each problem below. Glue the correct solution picture next to each problem. Talk about it.

1. You and your brother both want a cookie but there is only one left.

Glue

2. You have a spelling test tomorrow, but you left your spelling book at school.

Glue

3. You cannot find the book you need at the library.

Glue

4. Your baby brother is crying in his crib.

Glue

5. Your cat is lost.

Glue

Name _____   Homework Partner _____   Date _____

Game Board 5

What Should You Do?

#BK-308 Positive Pragmatic Game Boards Fun Sheets • ©2003 Super Duper® Publications • 1-800-277-8737 • Online! www.superduperinc.com

A Beautiful Ending

Instructions: Read/listen to the story below. Fill in each blank with a solution to the problem. _____

Yesterday was an awful day! It started when I woke up late. I was in such a hurry that I spilled milk on my homework, so

_____. Of course, I

missed the bus, so _____.

When I got to school, one of my friends started calling me names, so _____

_____.

When it was time for lunch I remembered that I had left my lunch at

home, so _____. At lunch, my

loose tooth fell out so _____.

During Math, I got in trouble for talking, so_____

_____.

Finally, my awful day was over. Oh no, it was not over! When I got home

from school, Mom was not there so _____

_____. Soon Mom came

home and I told her all about my awful day. Mom said I could have a snack. I

could not reach the cookie jar, so _____

_____. Mom just hugged

me and said, "I'll get the cookies for you. I love you."

I felt much better. Tomorrow is a new day. It will be a good day!

_____   _____   _____
Name   Homework Partner   Date

#BK-308 Positive Pragmatic Game Boards Fun Sheets • ©2003 Super Duper® Publications • 1-800-277-8737 • Online! www.superduperinc.com

71

Finding Problems

Instructions: Look at the picture pairs below. Only one picture in each pair shows a problem. Color the picture that shows a problem. State the problem aloud. Tell how you would solve the problem.

Game Board 5

What Should You Do?

_____ _____ _____
Name   Homework Partner   Date

What Caused the Problem?

Instructions: Look at the pictures on the left. Describe each problem. Draw a line from the problem on the left to the cause of the problem on the right. Tell what you would do in each situation.

Name

Homework Partner

Date

Spin a Problem

Instructions: If you prefer, glue this page to construction paper for added durability. Cut out the arrow/dial. Use a brad to connect the dial to the circle. Spin the spinner. Read/talk about each problem and tell what you would do. _____

Name   Homework Partner   Date

Game Board 5

What Should You Do?

#BK-308 Positive Pragmatic Game Boards Fun Sheets • ©2003 Super Duper® Publications • 1-800-277-8737 • Online! www.superduperinc.com

Problem Solving Tic-Tac-Toe

Instructions: Cut out the Tic-Tac-Toe tokens below. One player gets "?'s" and the other gets "!'s". As you cover each square, read/talk about each problem and tell what you would do. Three in a row wins!

 You left your backpack on the school bus.	 You lost your library book.	 You notice that a stranger is talking to some children.
 You spilled milk on your homework paper.	 You found a gold ring on the school playground.	 You lost your house key.
It is a stormy night. Suddenly, the lights go out!	 At the supermarket, you accidentally drop and break a jar of tomato sauce.	 At a restaurant, your hamburger has ketchup on it. You did not want ketchup.

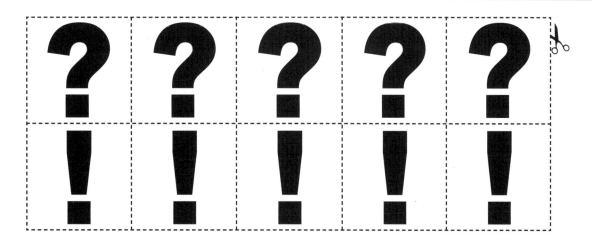

Name _____   Homework Partner _____   Date _____

Game Board 5

What Should You Do?

#BK-308 Positive Pragmatic Game Boards Fun Sheets • ©2003 Super Duper® Publications • 1-800-277-8737 • Online! www.superduperinc.com   75

What Could You Do?

Instructions: Read/listen to each problem below. Tell what you could do to avoid each problem. (Bonus: Can you think of a second way to avoid each problem?)

LOST
CAT

1. What could you do so you don't lose your house key?

2. What could you do so you don't leave your spelling book at school?

3. What could you do so you don't get lost at the mall?

4. What could you do so you don't leave your backpack on the bus?

5. What could you do so you don't lose your library book?

6. What could you do so you don't run out of glue?

7. What could you do so you don't break your mom's best vase?

8. What could you do so your cat does not get lost?

_____   _____   _____
Name   Homework Partner   Date

#BK-308 Positive Pragmatic Game Boards Fun Sheets • ©2003 Super Duper® Publications • 1-800-277-8737 • Online! www.superduperinc.com

Problems in the Neighborhood

Instructions: Find and color the following problems in the scene below: smoke coming from a house, a lost dog, a wallet on the sidewalk, a broken window, a child running after the bus, a girl calling a cat, a strange car following a child. State a solution for each problem.

Here Kitty!

SCHOOL BUS

Name _____

Homework Partner _____

Date _____

New Kid in Class

Instructions: There is a new student in your class. He doesn't know anyone. What are some things you can do? Say or write your ideas in the spaces below.

_____ _____ _____

Name   Homework Partner   Date

Game Board 5

What Should You Do?

    #BK-308 Positive Pragmatic Game Boards Fun Sheets • ©2003 Super Duper® Publications • 1-800-277-8737 • Online! www.superduperinc.com

Let's Act It Out

Instructions: If you prefer, glue this page to construction paper for added durability. Cut out the cards and place them face down on the table. Choose a card. With a partner, decide who will play the part of each character named on the card. Act out the problem described on the card and a possible solution. Continue until all cards are used.

Characters 1) Mom 2) Child **Problem** You broke your mom's best vase by mistake.	**Characters** 1) 911 Operator 2) Child **Problem** You see smoke coming from a neighbor's home.	**Characters** 1) Teacher 2) Child **Problem** You get in trouble for talking, but it was really the student behind you.
Characters 1) Little Brother 2) Child **Problem** Your little brother keeps taking your toys.	**Characters** 1) Librarian 2) Child **Problem** You lost your library book.	**Characters** 1) Friend 2) Child **Problem** One of your friends keeps calling you funny names.
Characters 1) Club Member 2) Child **Problem** Some kids start a club but they say you can't join.	**Characters** 1) New Student 2) Child **Problem** There is a new child in your class. She doesn't know anyone.	**Characters** 1) Friend 2) Child **Problem** You have a spelling test tomorrow and you left your spelling book at school.
Characters 1) Brother 2) Child **Problem** You have a flat tire on your bike and need to get to baseball practice.	**Characters** 1) Policeman 2) Child **Problem** You found a wallet on the sidewalk with lots of money in it.	**Characters** 1) Neighbor 2) Child **Problem** You broke your neighbor's window with a baseball.

_____   _____   _____
Name   Homework Partner   Date

Game Board 5

What Should You Do?

What is the Problem?

Instructions: Look at each picture below. Describe each problem. (Bonus: What would you do to solve each problem?) _____

Game Board 6

Feelings and Emotions

Make-a-Face Tic-Tac-Toe

Instructions: Cut out the Tic-Tac-Toe tokens below. One player gets "X's" and the other gets "O's." First player picks out a square, makes a face showing the feeling indicated on the square, and covers the square with his/her token. The second player follows in turn. Three in a row wins!

Happy	**Sad**	**Angry**
Embarrassed	**Scared**	**Puzzled**
Surprised	**Disappointed**	**Proud**

_____   _____   _____
Name   Homework Partner   Date

   #BK-308 Positive Pragmatic Game Boards Fun Sheets • ©2003 Super Duper® Publications • 1-800-277-8737 • Online! www.superduperinc.com

You Should Be Proud!

Instructions: Glue this page onto construction paper for added durability. Everyone has something to be proud of! Write down on the ribbon below some of the reasons you feel proud. Color the ribbon and cut it out. Wear your ribbon with pride!

I am proud because...

_____

_____

_____

_____

_____

_____   _____   _____
Name   Homework Partner   Date   **Feelings**

Feelings Sort

Instructions: Cut the slot at the top of each feeling box. Then, cut out the cards on page 85. Place all the cards face down on the table. Choose a card and read the situation. Place each card in the box with the feeling that goes with the situation.

#BK-308 Positive Pragmatic Game Boards Fun Sheets • ©2003 Super Duper® Publications • 1-800-277-8737 • Online! www.superduperinc.com

Game Board 6

Feelings

_____   _____   _____
Name   Homework Partner   Date

Feelings Sort Cards

Instructions: Cut out the cards on the dotted lines. Follow the directions on page 84.

Your brother borrows your bike and rips the seat.	You hear a loud clap of thunder.	Your brother spilled milk on your homework.
Your best friend is moving away.	You won the poetry contest at your school.	Your pet frog died.
A stranger offers you a ride.	The school bully knocks all of your books out of your hands.	You think someone is following you.
Your grandma is in the hospital.	Your mom takes you to the pet store to buy a puppy.	You are going to an amusement park for your birthday party.

Game Board 6

Feelings

_____   _____   _____
Name   Homework Partner   Date

Feeling Match Up

Instructions: Look at the faces of the children on the left. Draw a line to connect the child to the thing that might have caused the expression on the child's face.

Game Board 6

Name   Homework Partner   Date   **Feelings**

 #BK-308 Positive Pragmatic Game Boards Fun Sheets • ©2003 Super Duper® Publications • 1-800-277-8737 • Online! www.superduperinc.com

The Happiest Day of My Life

Instructions: Answer each question in a full sentence. _____

When was the happiest day of your life? _____

_____

Who were you with? _____

Where were you? _____

Why was it the happiest day? _____

_____

Write down all your answers to form a story. Read your story aloud.

The Happiest Day of My Life

_____

_____

_____

_____

_____

_____

_____

_____

| Name | Homework Partner | Date | **Feelings** |

Game Board 6

Fill in a Feeling

Instructions: Read/listen to each sentence below.   Then complete each sentence.

1. Mom said that I could not go to the park today. I felt _____
   _____.

2. I got all A's on my report card. I felt _____
   _____.

3. My pet hamster died. I felt _____.

4. My parents decided to take me to the circus. I felt _____
   _____.

5. My friend called me a "baby." I felt _____
   _____.

6. I heard strange noises at night. I felt _____
   _____.

7. I won the first prize trophy in the spelling bee. I felt _____
   _____.

8. I got in trouble in front of the whole class. I felt _____
   _____.

9. It was the first day of school. I felt _____
   _____.

10. It was the last day of school. I felt _____
   _____.

			Game Board 6
Name	Homework Partner	Date	**Feelings**

#BK-308 Positive Pragmatic Game Boards Fun Sheets • ©2003 Super Duper® Publications • 1-800-277-8737 • Online! www.superduperinc.com

Feelings Scrapbook

Instructions: Cut out the scrapbook pages along the dotted lines on pages 89-91. Place the cover on top and staple the pages together where indicated. Have fun filling out your scrapbook.

HAPPY

Things That Make Me Happy . . . .

_____

_____

_____

_____

_____

(Draw yourself or paste a photo of yourself with a happy face.)

What does your face look like when you are happy? _____

_____

SAD

Things That Make Me Sad . . . .

_____

_____

_____

_____

_____

(Draw yourself or paste a photo of yourself with a sad face.)

What does your face look like when you are sad? _____

_____

_____   _____   _____   Game Board 6

Name   Homework Partner   Date   **Feelings**

Feelings Scrapbook (cont.)

Instructions: Cut out the pages along the dotted lines. Place the cover on top and staple the pages together. Have fun filling out your scrapbook. _____

A n g R Y

Things That Make Me Angry . . . .

_____

_____

_____

_____

_____

(Draw yourself or paste a photo of yourself with an angry face.)

What does your face look like when you are angry? _____

_____

S C A R E D

Things That Make Me Scared . . . .

_____

_____

_____

_____

_____

(Draw yourself or paste a photo of yourself with a scared face.)

What does your face look like when you are scared? _____

_____

| Name | Homework Partner | Date | Game Board 6 **Feelings** |

#BK-308 Positive Pragmatic Game Boards Fun Sheets • ©2003 Super Duper® Publications • 1-800-277-8737 • Online! www.superduperinc.com

Feelings Scrapbook (cont.)

Instructions: Cut out the pages along the dotted lines. Place the cover on top and staple the pages together. Have fun filling out your scrapbook. _____

S U R P R I S E D

Things That Make Me Surprised . . . .

_____

_____

_____

_____

_____

(Draw yourself or paste a photo of yourself with a surprised face.)

What does your face look like when you are surprised? _____

_____

staple

My Feelings
S c r a p b o o k

staple

Game Board 6

| Name | Homework Partner | Date | Feelings |

Paste-a-Feeling Face

Instructions: Cut out the "feeling faces" below. Read each sentence and glue, tape/place each "feeling face" in the box next to each sentence. Talk about why you would have each feeling.

1. You are alone and you hear a strange noise.

2. Your brother jumps out from behind the bedroom door.

3. You sit down and split your pants.

4. Your pet just died.

5. You got an A+ on your book report.

6. Your sister borrowed your new shirt and got ink all over it.

surprised sad happy mad embarrassed scared

_____ _____ _____

Name Homework Partner Date

Game Board 6

Feelings

#BK-308 Positive Pragmatic Game Boards Fun Sheets • ©2003 Super Duper® Publications • 1-800-277-8737 • Online! www.superduperinc.com

Feelings Spinner

Instructions: If you prefer, glue this page to construction paper for added durability. Cut out the arrow/dial. Use a brad to connect the dial to the circle. Spin the spinner. Follow the instructions on the space.

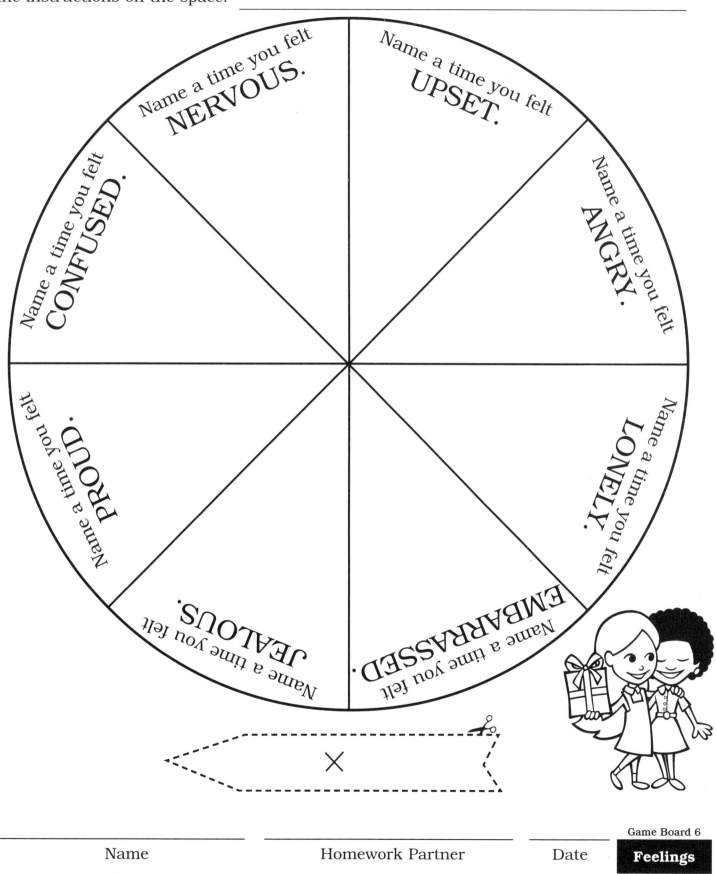

#BK-308 Positive Pragmatic Game Boards Fun Sheets • ©2003 Super Duper® Publications • 1-800-277-8737 • Online! www.superduperinc.com

93

Make-a-Face Mask

Instructions: Glue this mask on to construction paper for added durability. Cut out the faces on page 95. Choose the face you would like, and glue, tape/place it on the mask. Cut out the eyes. Hold your mask up to your face and tell how you are feeling. Why do you feel that way? _____

_____ _____ _____ Game Board 6

Name　　　　　　Homework Partner　　　　Date　　　**Feelings**

Make-a-Face Facial Expressions

See instructions on previous page.

Name   Homework Partner   Date

Game Board 6

Feelings

Feelings Crossword

Instructions: Complete the crossword puzzle by choosing a feeling for each clue. Use the Word Bank below.

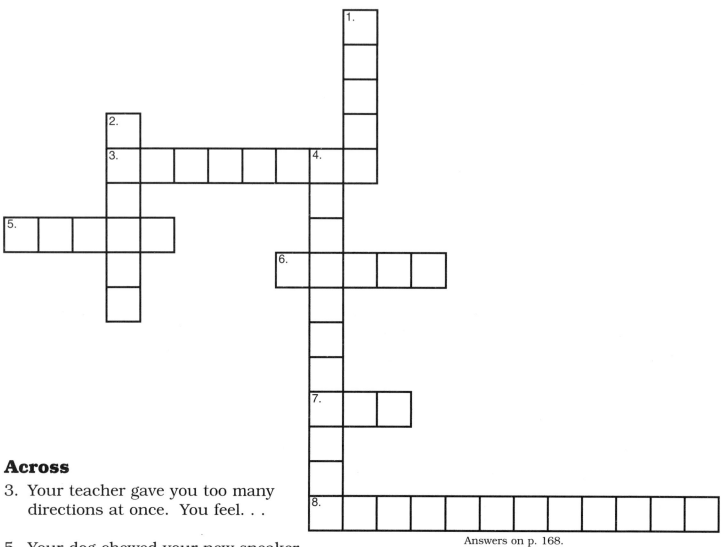

Answers on p. 168.

Across

3. Your teacher gave you too many directions at once. You feel. . .

5. Your dog chewed your new sneaker. You feel. . .

6. You won a stuffed animal at the carnival. You feel. . .

7. Your cat ran away. You feel. . .

8. Your friend can't sleep over because he's sick. You feel. . .

Down

1. You were chosen "Student of the Week." You feel. . .

2. The biggest kid in school picks a fight with you. You feel. . .

4. You dropped your lunch tray. You feel. . .

Word Bank

confused   embarrassed   happy   scared   proud   angry   disappointed   sad

---

Name   Homework Partner   Date

Feelings Synonyms

Instructions: Read each sentence. Choose a synonym (word that has the *same* meaning) for the underlined word from the Word Bank below. Write the correct synonym in the blank following each sentence. Now re-read each sentence using the synonym.

1. Jane was <u>happy</u> because she was going on a vacation _____

2. My brother made me so <u>angry</u> when he broke my new toy. _____

3. I was <u>surprised</u> when my Mom told me school would be closed tomorrow.

   _____

4. My class trip was canceled. I was so <u>sad</u>. _____

5. Mary was <u>scared</u> during the thunderstorm. _____

6. After Mr. Jones gave us directions, I felt very <u>puzzled</u>. _____

7. Jack was <u>nervous</u> because he had to sing in front of the whole class. _____

8. No one wanted to play with Juan. He felt so <u>lonely</u>. _____

9. My little brother got a new bike. I was <u>jealous</u> of him. _____

Word Bank

alone	frightened	unhappy
anxious	furious	glad
shocked	envious	confused

Answers on p. 168.

_____   _____   _____   Game Board 6
Name   Homework Partner   Date   **Feelings**

Create-a-Card

Instructions: Your friend is sad, so you are going to make a card to cheer him/her up. Cut out the card on the dotted lines. Fold the card in half, so only pages 2 and 3 are visible. Fold the card in half again, from left to right, so that the "Cheer-Up" cover is on the front of the card. Color and complete the card.

Created by _____

Cheer-Up

1 4
2 3

I'm glad you're my friend because

_____
_____
_____
_____
_____

From your friend,

_____

(Draw a picture of you and your friend doing something together.)

Name _____ Homework Partner _____ Date _____ **Feelings**

#BK-308 Positive Pragmatic Game Boards Fun Sheets • ©2003 Super Duper® Publications • 1-800-277-8737 • Online! www.superduperinc.com

MEOW!

Game Board 7

Idioms
What do these
really mean?

Using Figurative Language

Monkey Idioms

Instructions: Cut out the bananas at the bottom of the page. Read the idiom on each monkey. Find the banana that contains the correct meaning of each idiom. Glue/ tape or place the banana next to the correct monkey.

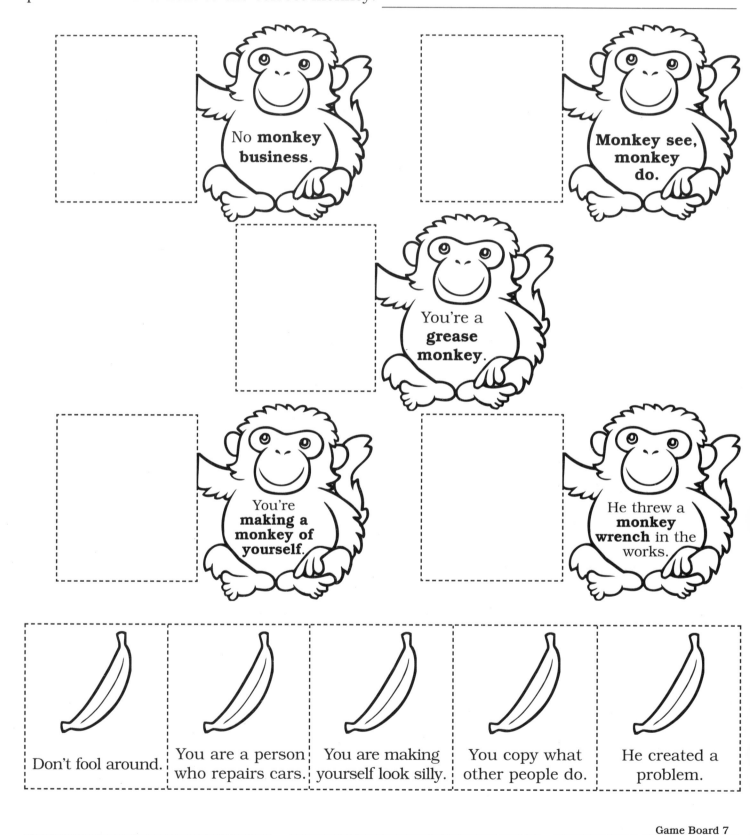

No **monkey business**.

Monkey see, monkey do.

You're a **grease monkey**.

You're **making a monkey of yourself**.

He threw a **monkey wrench** in the works.

Don't fool around.

You are a person who repairs cars.

You are making yourself look silly.

You copy what other people do.

He created a problem.

_____   _____   _____
Name   Homework Partner   Date

Game Board 7

Idioms

Feelings Idioms

Instructions: Draw a line to connect the idiom to the correct feeling. (*Challenge - Make up your own idiom.)

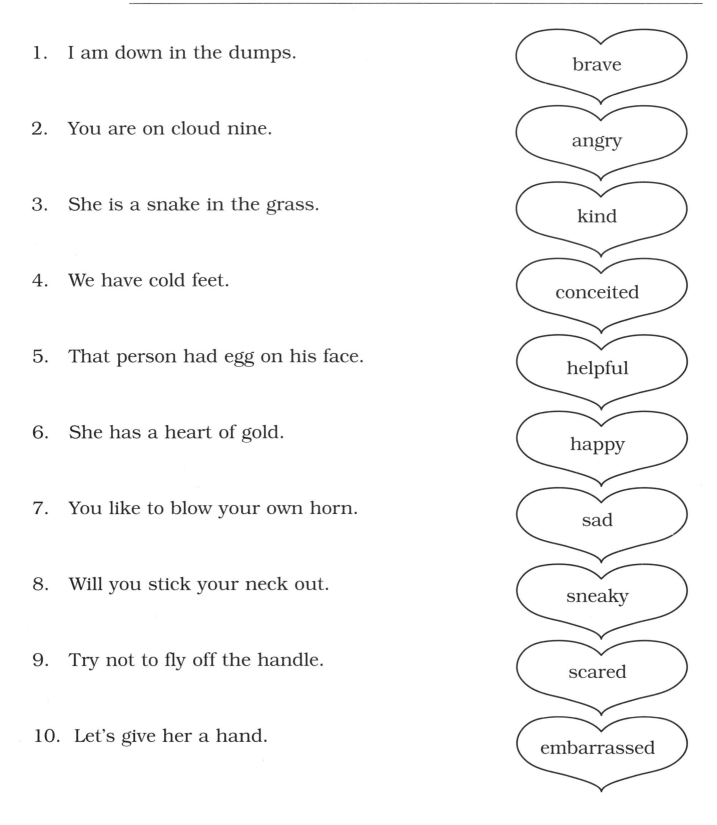

1. I am down in the dumps.

2. You are on cloud nine.

3. She is a snake in the grass.

4. We have cold feet.

5. That person had egg on his face.

6. She has a heart of gold.

7. You like to blow your own horn.

8. Will you stick your neck out.

9. Try not to fly off the handle.

10. Let's give her a hand.

brave

angry

kind

conceited

helpful

happy

sad

sneaky

scared

embarrassed

_____   _____   _____   Game Board 7
Name   Homework Partner   Date

Idioms

School Days

Instructions: Cut out the pages of the book on pages 102-103. Staple the pages where indicated. As you read each story, give the meaning of the underlined idioms.

STAPLE
STAPLE

It was Monday morning. I got up on the wrong side of the bed.

1

I was hungry. I poured out a huge bowl of cereal. My eyes were bigger than my stomach.

2

Toot! Toot! Oh no, the bus! I had to shake a leg.

3

I caught the bus and got to school just in time to see Mr. Jones, the principal. He's as tough as nails!

4

_____   _____   _____
Name   Homework Partner   Date

#BK-308 Positive Pragmatic Game Boards Fun Sheets • ©2003 Super Duper® Publications • 1-800-277-8737 • Online! www.superduperinc.com

School Days (cont.)

Instructions: Follow the instructions on page 102. _____

I got to class and decided to <u>put my best foot forward</u>. I really wanted to have a good day.

5

My teacher, Mrs. May, told me that my book report was the best in the class. I was <u>on top of the world</u>!

6

At lunch, Susie told me that she was <u>nuts about me</u>! I was <u>on cloud nine</u>!

7

The afternoon went very quickly. When Mrs. May said it was time to go home, I thought <u>she was pulling my leg</u>. I guess <u>time flies</u> when you're having fun!

8

_____ _____ _____
Name   Homework Partner   Date

Game Board 7

Idioms

Put Your Foot Down

Instructions: Cut out the sneakers at the bottom of the page. Glue/tape or place the sneakers on the octopus. Each time you do this, tell what the idiom means.

You put your best foot forward.

I have two left feet.

The shoe is on the other foot.

You put your foot in your mouth.

You put your foot down.

I have a foot in the door.

You drag your feet.

I have cold feet.

Name   Homework Partner   Date

Color a Bug

Instructions: Read each idiom and its meaning. If the meaning is correct, color the happy bug. If the meaning is incorrect, color the sad bug and tell your helper the correct meaning. _____

1. <u>Don't bug me</u> means. . . there are a lot of bugs in the house.

2. <u>Knock it off</u> means. . . to knock things off a table.

3. To <u>monkey around</u> means. . . to fool around.

4. To be <u>on thin ice</u> means. . . to be in a dangerous situation.

5. <u>Time flies</u> means. . . that the clock is flying across the room.

6. You are <u>pulling someone's leg</u> means. . . you are wrestling with someone.

7. You don't <u>see eye to eye</u> means. . . you do not agree.

8. Your <u>eyes are bigger than your stomach</u> means. . . you have very big eyes.

_____   _____   _____
          Name   Homework Partner   Date

Game Board 7

Idioms

#BK-308 Positive Pragmatic Game Boards Fun Sheets • ©2003 Super Duper® Publications • 1-800-277-8737 • Online! www.superduperinc.com

Idiom Sentence Completion

Instructions: Fill in each blank with an idiom from the Word Bank below.

1. We had better _____.

   If we don't, we'll be late for dinner at your grandma's house.

2. I can never fool my mom. She has _____.

3. I have been busy all day, so please _____.

4. Mary is such a kind and caring girl. She has _____.

5. John has such a beautiful garden. He has _____.

6. My teacher is very strict. She is _____.

7. When it comes to building model cars, I'm _____.

8. It's getting very late and I have to go to work in the morning. I have to _____

   _____.

9. John never listens to his Mom. Whatever she says goes _____

   _____.

10. I was _____ when I lost the contest.

Word Bank

eyes in the back of her head	down in the dumps
a green thumb	give me a break
as tough as nails	a heart of gold
hit the sack	all thumbs
in one ear and out the other	shake a leg

In a Pickle

Instructions: Cut out the pickles at the bottom of the page. Cut out the slot on the pickle jar. Put a pickle in the jar **only** if the idiom on the pickle is something that might put you in a pickle (get you in trouble or in a bad situation). You are/Your...

...in the hot seat.

...up the creek.

...on cloud nine.

...in the doghouse.

...a dead duck.

...up against the wall.

...in over your head.

...hitting the jackpot.

...goose is cooked.

...on thin ice.

...name is mud.

...walking on air.

Game Board 7

Idioms

Name　　　　Homework Partner　　　　Date

Idiom Memory

Instructions: If you prefer, glue this page to construction paper for added durability. Cut out all of the cards, shuffle and place them in A and B piles face down. Take turns flipping two cards and trying to find matches. Try to match each idiom card with its real meaning. The player with the most matches wins! _____

You're in the Doghouse

Instructions: Cut out the dogs at the bottom of the page. Read the idiom on each dog. If the idiom tells about something that might put you in the doghouse (get you in trouble), glue/tape or place the dog inside the doghouse. If the idiom tells about something that won't put you in the doghouse, glue/tape or place it outside the doghouse.

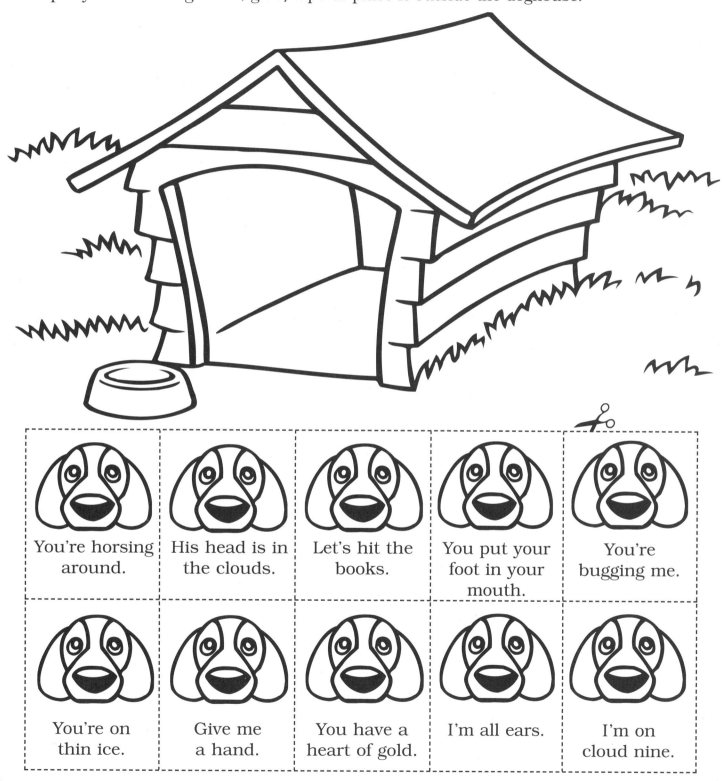

You're horsing around.

His head is in the clouds.

Let's hit the books.

You put your foot in your mouth.

You're bugging me.

You're on thin ice.

Give me a hand.

You have a heart of gold.

I'm all ears.

I'm on cloud nine.

Name _____ Homework Partner _____ Date _____

Game Board 7

Idioms

Write an Idiom

Instructions: Read each sentence aloud. Rewrite each sentence substituting the idiom from the Word Bank below for the underlined words. _____

Example: It's raining <u>very hard</u>.
            It's raining <u>cats and dogs</u>.

1. It's time to <u>get going</u>. _____

2. I want you to <u>stop what you're doing</u>. _____

3. You are <u>in serious trouble</u>. _____

4. He's <u>very happy</u>. _____

5. He <u>really likes you</u>! _____

6. Mike <u>is feeling nervous</u>. _____

Word Bank

cut it out	is nuts about you
has butterflies in his stomach	in hot water
hit the road	on top of the world

When Did It Happen to You?

Instructions: Cut out the game markers below. Flip a coin to determine the number of spaces to move. Heads moves one space. Tails moves two spaces. Take turns moving around the board and telling about a time when you...

START

...lost your head.

...met someone who was as tough as nails.

...had two left feet.

...did not see eye to eye with someone.

...were on cloud nine.

...had eyes in the back of your head.

...hit the nail on the head.

...were head over heels over something.

...hit the sack.

...saw time fly.

...were in the doghouse.

...got up on the wrong side of the bed.

...were down in the dumps.

FINISH

...let the cat out of the bag.

...were on thin ice.

...put your foot in your mouth.

Game Board 7

Idioms

Animal Idiom Match

Instructions: If you prefer, glue this page to construction paper for added durability. Cut out all the cards, shuffle, and place them face down on the table. Take turns flipping two cards and trying to find a match. Tell what each idiom really means. The player keeps any matches. Play continues in turn. Player with the most matches wins!

 You are the **cat's meow**.

 You will **take the bull by the horns**.

 There's **a snake in the grass**.

 He really **got my goat**.

 I have a **frog in my throat**.

 Get off **your high horse**.

 She is really living **high off the hog**.

 We are on **a wild goose chase**.

Name   Homework Partner   Date

Game Board 7

Idioms

#BK-308 Positive Pragmatic Game Boards Fun Sheets • ©2003 Super Duper® Publications • 1-800-277-8737 • Online! www.superduperinc.com

Ms. Idiom

Instructions: Cut out the body parts at the bottom of the page. Next, look at the idioms on the right and left of the body. Say/write the correct body part in each blank to complete each idiom. Then, glue/tape or place that body part on Ms. Idiom.

My _____ are bigger than my stomach.

You have a _____ of gold.

You have a green _____.

I have a frog in my _____.

Keep your _____ to the grindstone.

I'm all _____.

I have butterflies in my _____.

Zip your _____.

You put your _____ in your mouth.

You have a chip on your _____.

Give me a _____.

Put your best _____ forward.

Surprise Party!

Instructions: Read the story below. Underline the idioms in the story and tell what each idiom means. (Hint: You should find ten idioms.)

"Mary is going to be so surprised," said Joey as he tried to hang a long piece of crepe paper.

"We've been planning this surprise party for weeks," said Charlie.

"If anyone spills the beans, they're going to be in hot water," replied Joey sharply.

Joey struggled with the crepe paper.

"Charlie, could you please give me a hand? I can't decorate! I'm all thumbs!" whined Joey.

"We'd better shake a leg. Mary will be here soon," said Charlie.

"Don't worry, boys," replied Mom. "It's raining cats and dogs out there. I'm sure Mary will be a little late!"

"Mother, when is everyone coming?" asked Charlie.

"They should be here soon," said Mom.

Ding Dong! Joey ran to the window.

"Hide, it's Mary!" whispered Joey.

"You are so full of baloney," laughed Charlie.

"You're right," said Joey. "It's Aunt Mary, Uncle Mike and some of Mary's friends from school."

Charlie went to the door to let the guests in.

"You guys better stop monkeying around," scolded Mom. "Mary should be here soon."

"Charlie, I just heard a car door," said Joey as he crawled over to the window. "Turn out the lights and zip your lips. . . it's Mary! This party is going to knock her socks off."

Ding Dong!

"Surprise!"

Answers on p. 168.

Name _____ Homework Partner _____ Date _____

#BK-308 Positive Pragmatic Game Boards Fun Sheets • ©2003 Super Duper® Publications • 1-800-277-8737 • Online! www.superduperinc.com

Game Board 8

What Should You Do Instead of...?

Appropriate Interaction

Crazy Classroom

Instructions: Find and circle the things the children should not be doing in the silly scene below. Tell what each child should be doing instead. How many did you find? (eight)

Name _____   Homework Partner _____   Date _____

The Best Thing To Do

Instructions: Read the sentence starters below. Color the star next to the sentence that best completes each sentence starter. _____

1. Instead of taking glue from your friend's desk...

   ☆ Take glue from your teacher's desk.

   ☆ Do not do the assignment.

   ☆ Ask your friend if you may borrow his glue.

2. Instead of having a tantrum because you don't get what you want...

   ☆ Go to your room and pout.

   ☆ Take a deep breath and count to ten.

   ☆ Keep saying, "I want it. I want it. I want it!"

3. Instead of ignoring your dad when he tells you to do something ...

   ☆ Tell your dad to just wait a minute.

   ☆ Tell your dad you are too busy.

   ☆ Do what your dad says.

4. Instead of asking Mom a question while she is on the phone...

   ☆ Tug on Mom's arm.

   ☆ Wait patiently until Mom is off the phone.

   ☆ Tell Mom to get off the phone now.

5. Instead of telling a classmate that she can't be in your club...

   ☆ Tell her to go start her own club.

   ☆ Tell her your club is only for your best friends.

   ☆ Let her be in your club to see if she likes it.

Game Board 8

What Should You Do Instead of...

_____   _____   _____

Name   Homework Partner   Date

#BK-308 Positive Pragmatic Game Boards Fun Sheets • ©2003 Super Duper® Publications • 1-800-277-8737 • Online! www.superduperinc.com

Cut and Paste Fun

Instructions: Cut out the pictures at the bottom of the page. Read each sentence below. Glue/tape or place the picture that best completes each sentence in the correct box. Tell what you should do instead.

1. Instead of calling out in class, you should. . .

2. Instead of having a running race down the hallway, you should. . .

3. Instead of pushing someone off the slide so you can use it, you should. . .

4. Instead of hogging all the toys, you should. . .

5. Instead of reaching across someone's plate to get the milk, you should. . .

Name

Homework Partner

Date

Wrong to Right

Instructions: Match each inappropriate picture on the left to an appropriate picture on the right. Describe each picture.

Name   Homework Partner   Date

Manner Park

Instructions: Circle the children who are having good manners at the park. Put an X on the children who are not having good manners. Talk about the pictures.

Name _____

Homework Partner _____

Date _____

#BK-308 Positive Pragmatic Game Boards Fun Sheets • ©2003 Super Duper® Publications • 1-800-277-8737 • Online! www.superduperinc.com

Memory Game Fun

Instructions: If you prefer, glue this page on to construction paper for added durability. Cut out all of the cards and place them face down on the table. The first player turns over a card, talks about it, and tells if the scene shows appropriate or inappropriate behavior. The player then turns over a second card, trying to match the appropriate picture with the inappropriate picture. The player keeps any matches. Play continues in turn. The most matches wins!

#BK-308 Positive Pragmatic Game Boards Fun Sheets • ©2003 Super Duper® Publications • 1-800-277-8737 • Online! www.superduperinc.com

Sorting Fun

Instructions: Cut a slot on the dotted lines on the garbage can and on the ribbon. Cut out the picture cards on page 123. Choose a card. Talk about the picture. If the child is having good manners, put the card in the ribbon slot. If the child is acting inappropriately, put it in the garbage can and tell what the child should do instead.

PLACE

1ST

Name

Homework Partner

Date

Sorting Fun

Instructions: Cut out the cards below and follow the instructions on page 122.

Lunch Time

Instructions: Follow the path to the cafeteria. As you move along, talk about each picture. What would you do if you saw these things?

Name _____

Homework Partner _____

Date _____

Instead Spinner Fun

Instructions: If you prefer, glue this page to construction paper for added durability. Cut out the arrow/dial. Use a brad to connect the dial to the circle. Spin the spinner. Describe the picture, read the words in the bubble, and tell what you would do/say instead.

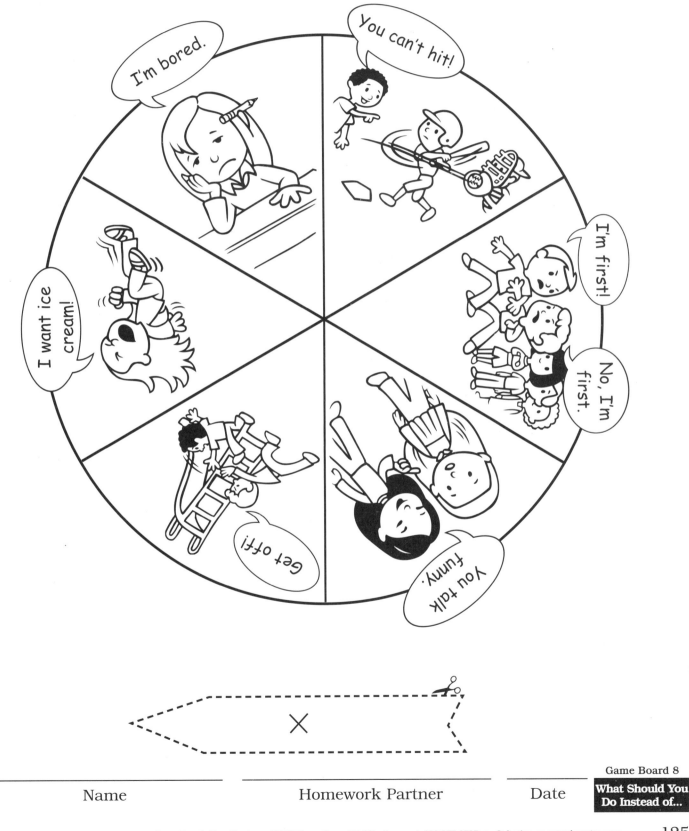

#BK-308 Positive Pragmatic Game Boards Fun Sheets • ©2003 Super Duper® Publications • 1-800-277-8737 • Online! www.superduperinc.com   125

Appropriate Penguin

Instructions: Cut out the penguin below. Then, follow the directions on page 127.

Glue
booklet
here.

Appropriate Penguin

Instructions: Cut on the dotted lines below. Stack the pages in order and staple as indicated. Glue your booklet onto the penguin on page 126. Talk about each picture. Next, tell what the penguin should do to have good behavior. _____

Name _____   Homework Partner _____   Date _____

Instead Tic-Tac-Toe

Instructions: Cut out the Tic-Tac-Toe tokens below. One player gets "X's" and the other gets "O's." Player One picks out a square, and talks about the picture. The player tells what the person should do to have good behavior. The player then puts a token on the square. Player Two follows in turn. Three in a row wins!

#BK-308 Positive Pragmatic Game Boards Fun Sheets • ©2003 Super Duper® Publications • 1-800-277-8737 • Online! www.superduperinc.com

Why Shouldn't You?

Instructions: Write or tell the answer to each "Why" question below. Then write or tell what you should do instead. _____

Why shouldn't you. . .

1.   ...have a running race down the hallway? _____

_____.

   ...Instead, you should _____.

2.   ...go to a friend's house after school without your mom knowing? _____

_____.

   Instead, you should _____.

3.   ...quit because you are losing the game? _____

_____.

   Instead, you should _____.

4.   ...say, "Get out of here!" when your little brother wants to play with

   you?_____.

   Instead, you should _____.

5.   ...talk to your friend while your teacher is teaching? _____

_____.

   Instead, you should _____.

6.   ...talk and laugh during a fire drill? _____

_____.

   Instead, you should _____.

Susie Super Sitter

Instructions: Read or listen to the story on pages 130-131. Fill in (write or say) each blank with something you should do instead!

It was Susie's first time babysitting the four Baxter children. Mrs. Baxter said, "Susie, the kids can watch TV and have a snack before bed. Be good, kids! Good luck, Susie!"

Well, Susie soon had her hands full. "Excuse me kids," she said, "but that TV show is inappropriate! What can you watch instead?" "How about _____ _____?" Brenda suggested. "Great," said Susie. "Now, I'll go get your snack."

Susie came back with a carton of ice cream. Billy and Bobby scooped all of the ice cream into their bowls. None for Brenda and Belinda! "Oh Billy and Bobby, what should you do instead of eating all the ice cream?" Susie asked. "Well, I guess we should _____ _____," said Bobby. "It's all your fault, Bobby!" yelled Billy as he tackled his brother. "Wait just a minute," exclaimed Susie. "What should you two do instead of fighting?" she asked. "Well, I guess we should _____," replied Billy.

Name   Homework Partner   Date

Game Board 8

What Should You Do Instead of...

#BK-308 Positive Pragmatic Game Boards Fun Sheets • ©2003 Super Duper® Publications • 1-800-277-8737 • Online! www.superduperinc.com

Susie Super Sitter (cont.)

Instructions: Follow the instructions on page 130. _____

Finally, it was bedtime. "No, not yet!" "Just a minute!" "I'm not going!" "No fair."

Susie said, "Listen, kids! I said bedtime! What should you do instead of stalling?" The kids answered, "Okay, I guess we should _____." "That's better," said Susie. "I'll take this empty ice cream carton outside to the garbage can."

As soon as Susie went outside, the kids locked the door! "Kids, you know what you should do instead of locking me out!" The Baxters thought for awhile and said, "You're right, Susie. We should _____." And they did.

"Well," sighed Susie, "my babysitting days are over after tonight. Hmmm, let's see. What can I do instead of babysitting?"

Balloons for Sale

Instructions: Read/listen to the situation in each balloon. Color the balloons with good behavior situations green. Color the balloons with poor behavior situations yellow. For the poor behavior balloons, tell what you should have done. _____

You wander away from your mom at the store.

You say "Please pass the milk, Mom."

You wait patiently for Mom to get off the phone.

You ask Mom before going to a friend's house after school.

You cut in front of someone in line.

Your friend cannot shoot well, so you kick him off your basketball team.

Game Board 9

What Would You Say?

Greetings and Politeness Markers

Bubble Cut and Paste

Instructions: Cut out the answer bubbles at the bottom of the page. Look at each picture below and read/listen to each conversation bubble. Glue/tape or place the correct response in the empty bubble. Throw away the answers that are not appropriate.

Which is Better?

Instructions: Look at each picture on the left. Then, read or listen to the sentence next to it. Look at the pictures on the right and color the best answer. _____

 "You are late."	If you arrive late for practice, you should say...	 "Sorry coach!"	 "Chill out!"
	If your classmates are blocking the doorway, you should say...	 "Move!"	 "Excuse me."
	If you want your friend to stay for dinner, you should say...	 "She's staying for dinner!"	 "Can Sally stay for dinner?"
 "I have to go away on business."	If your dad is leaving on a business trip, you should say...	 "Have a safe trip Dad."	 "Again? Why?"

_____   _____   _____

Name   Homework Partner   Date

Game Board 9

What Would You Say?

Pete and Randy

Instructions: Cut out the juggling pins below. Read each phrase. Glue/tape or place the polite juggling pins around Polite Pete. Glue/tape or place the rude juggling pins around Rude Randy.

Polite Pete

Rude Randy

Excuse me, please.

May I have some?

Now what do you want?

Get out of my way.

May I help you?

I don't care for cake.

Give me that now!

I hate chocolate cake.

Have a good day, Mom!

_____   _____   _____
Name   Homework Partner   Date

What Would You Say?

Talking to Adults

Instructions: Look at each picture on the left. Read or listen to the two conversation bubbles on the right. Then, circle the bubble that has the better thing to say in each situation.

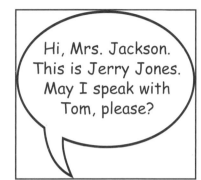

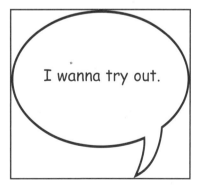

Dinner Time Fun

Instructions: Look at the dinner time scene below. Color the conversation bubbles that show good manners. Cross out the ones that show poor manners.

Name _____   Homework Partner _____   Date _____

Greetings!

Instructions: Read the description of each person below the line. Choose a greeting from the Word Bank that would be appropriate for each person described. (Some may be interchangeable.)

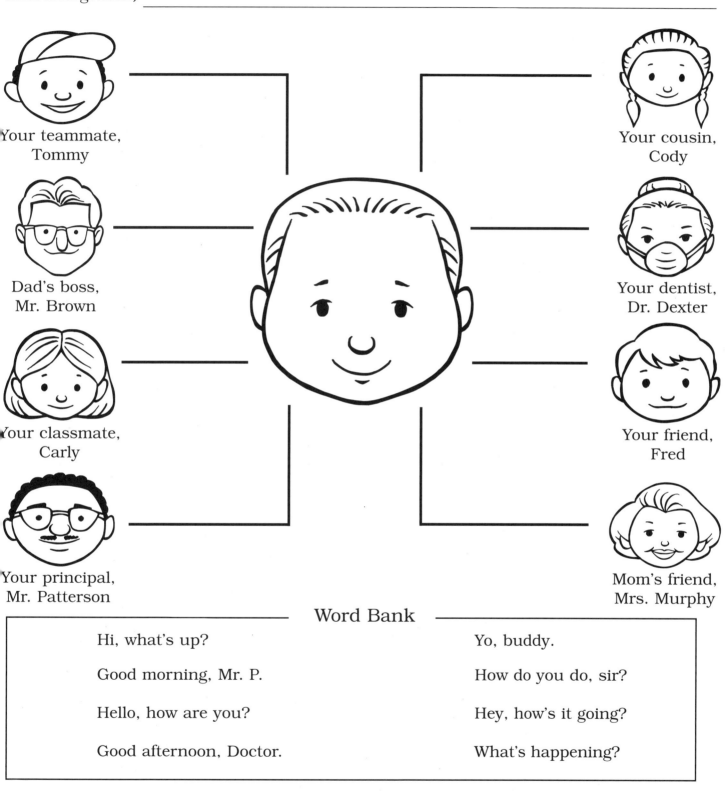

Your teammate, Tommy

Dad's boss, Mr. Brown

Your classmate, Carly

Your principal, Mr. Patterson

Your cousin, Cody

Your dentist, Dr. Dexter

Your friend, Fred

Mom's friend, Mrs. Murphy

Word Bank

Hi, what's up?

Good morning, Mr. P.

Hello, how are you?

Good afternoon, Doctor.

Yo, buddy.

How do you do, sir?

Hey, how's it going?

What's happening?

Name   Homework Partner   Date

Game Board 9

What Would You Say?

Getting Attention Tic-Tac-Toe

Instructions: Cut out the Tic-Tac-Toe tokens below. One player gets "X's" and the other gets "O's." Player One chooses a picture and tells if the situation is polite or rude. (If it is rude, tell how the child should act politely.) Player One covers the picture with a token. Player Two follows in turn. Three in a row wins!

Name   Homework Partner   Date

Game Board 9

What Would You Say?

140   #BK-308 Positive Pragmatic Game Boards Fun Sheets • ©2003 Super Duper® Publications • 1-800-277-8737 • Online! www.superduperinc.com

What Would You Say?

Instructions: Read each situation on the left. Draw a line to each situation on the right that has the thing you should say. _____

1. You need to interrupt
   two teachers talking.

2. You hurt a friend's feelings.

3. You do not care for any
   ice cream.

4. Your friend's mom had
   a new baby.

5. You would like more lemonade.

6. You want to introduce
   Sue to your mom.

7. A new girl has joined
   the computer club.

"Welcome."

"Congratulations!"

"Excuse me."

"I'm sorry."

"No, thank you."

*"May I have some
more please?"*

*"Mom, I'd like you to
meet Sue."*

Game Board 9

_____ _____ _____   **What Would**
Name   Homework Partner   Date   **You Say?**

It's Nice to Meet You!

Instructions: Cut out the sentence strips below. Sam wants to introduce Mary and John. Read each sentence strip at the bottom of the page. Look at each picture. Glue/tape or place the appropriate sentence strip below each picture. _____

"Here comes John! Hi John!"

"Hi Sam."

"I'd like you to meet Mary."
"Mary, this is John."

"It's nice to meet you, Mary."
"Same here, John."

"Let's all go to the park!"

_____   _____   _____   Game Board 9

Name   Homework Partner   Date   **What Would You Say?**

Fill In Fun!

Instructions: Complete each sentence with a polite word or phrase. Use the Word Bank below for hints. _____

1. May I have the orange juice, _____?

2. _____ for your help.

3. _____ that I hurt your feelings.

4. _____ have a cookie?

5. _____ to your new neighborhood.

6. You won the spelling bee! _____!

7. I have finished my dinner. _____?

8. _____ Mrs. Jones. It is nice to see you.

9. I'll see you tomorrow. _____.

Word Bank

May I be excused	Hello	Goodbye
May I	Welcome	Congratulations
Thank you	please	I'm sorry

Lotto Board Game

Instructions: Make a copy of the lotto board below for each child. Cut a piece of construction paper into 1″ x 1″ squares to use as markers. Then, follow the instructions on page 145.

I'm sorry.	Thank you.	Please.
Excuse me.	Good night.	Hello.
Goodbye.	Welcome.	Congratulations.

Lotto Calling Cards

Instructions: If you prefer, glue this page to construction paper for added durability. Cut out the cards. Place them in a paper bag. Player One chooses a card and reads or listens to the situation. He/she then places a marker on the polite word or phrase on his/her lotto board that fits the situation. Return the card to the paper bag. Player Two follows in turn. First player to complete his/her board wins. (Variations: First to get three in a row, or four corners wins.)

You have a new child in your class.	Your brother is going to bed early.	Your aunt and uncle are going home after having dinner with you.	You see your best friend on the playground.	You are hungry when you get home from school.
You need to borrow a pencil.	You need to interrupt your parents' conversation in an emergency.	Three of your friends are blocking the doorway and you need to pass.	You need help finding a library book.	Your dad is leaving for a business trip.
Your dad gives you your allowance.	You have a new family in your neighborhood.	You dial the wrong number.	You hurt your best friend's feelings.	Your friend tells you she likes your dress.
Your sister graduated from college.	You see your principal in the hallway.	You come home and see your mom and her new friend having tea.	Your bus driver drops you off at school.	Your brother won first prize in a talent show.

_____   _____   _____
Name   Homework Partner   Date

Politeness Spin

Instructions: If you prefer, glue this page to construction paper for added durability. Cut out the arrow/dial. Use a brad to connect the dial to the circle. Spin the spinner. Complete each sentence with polite manners. _____

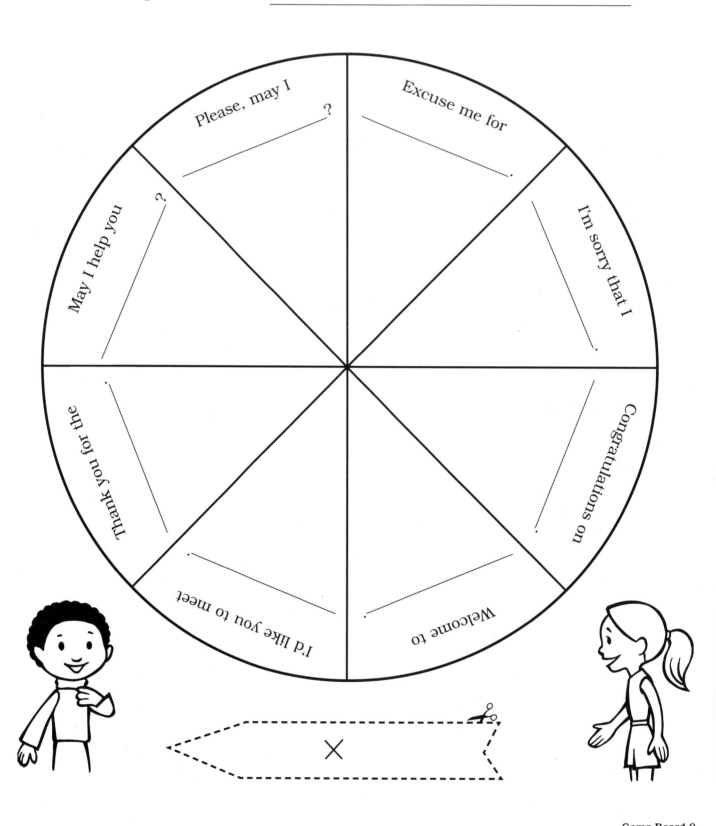

Please, may I _____ ?

Excuse me for _____ .

I'm sorry that I _____ .

May I help you _____ ?

Congratulations on _____ .

Thank you for the _____ .

I'd like you to meet _____ .

Welcome to _____ .

×

Polite Role Playing Fun

Instructions: If you prefer, glue this page to construction paper for added durability. Cut out the cards. Place all cards face down on the table. Player chooses a card and reads/listens to the situation. Players have fun acting out the situation with a partner. Continue until all situations have been acted out. _____

You see your principal in the hallway.	You arrive five minutes late for soccer practice.	Introduce yourself to your new teacher.	You see that your next door neighbor needs help carrying groceries into her house.	You need to borrow a pencil.
You dial the wrong number.	Your friend give you a birthday present you already have.	You need to leave the room during class.	Your cousin just graduated from high school.	You hurt your best friend's feelings.
You need help finding a library book.	You ask a policeman for directions.	Your sister is on the telephone and you need to make a call.	You have a new child in your class.	Your friend wants you to go to a movie but you already have plans.
You don't like the ice cream flavor your friend's mother offers you.	A friend thanks you for a birthday present.	Your teacher gave directions but you did not hear them.	Your mom is planting flowers and you want to help her.	A friend spills a glass of water on your kitchen floor.

_____ _____ _____ Game Board 9

Name　　　　　　　　　Homework Partner　　　　　Date

What Would You Say?

Silly School Day Spinner Story

Instructions: If you prefer, glue this page to construction paper for added durability. Cut out the arrow/dial. Use a brad to connect the dial to the circle. Then, read the instructions on page 149.

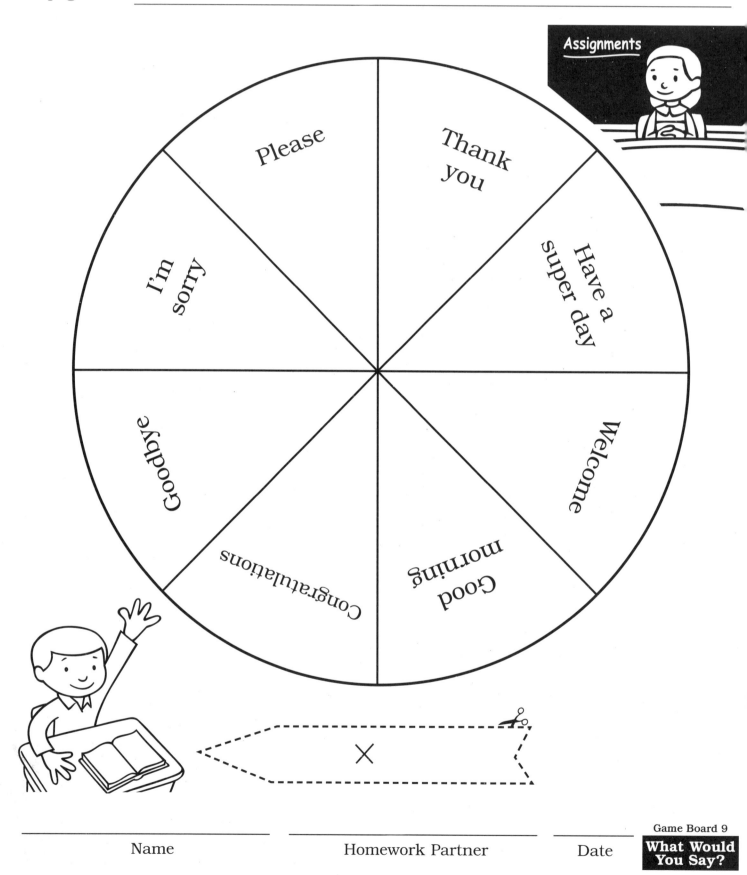

Name   Homework Partner   Date

Game Board 9

What Would You Say?

Silly School Day Spinner Story

Instructions: Read the story below. When you reach a blank, spin the spinner. Fill in the blank with that word. Read your silly story. Next, reread your story using the correct politeness words. _____

It was Monday morning. The school children heard

the voice of the principal, Miss Peterson, over the intercom.

"Attention _____, boys and

girls. _____ to you all.

Announcements for today are as follows: We had three winners in the math fair

this weekend. _____ to Mary, Matt, and Molly. We

have three new students today. A warm _____ to

Willy, Wanda, and Walter. _____ to say the cafeteria

will be closed today for repairs. Finally, we will be saying _____

_____ to Carlos the custodian today who is retiring after many

happy years. A job well done, Carlos!

_____ for your attention boys and girls and

_____."

Draw, Write, or Say Fun

Instructions: Draw, write, or talk about a situation in which you would use the polite words/phrases below. _____

"Excuse me."

"I'm sorry."

"Thank you."

"Please."

Name

Homework Partner

Date

Game Board 9

What Would You Say?

#BK-308 Positive Pragmatic Game Boards Fun Sheets • ©2003 Super Duper® Publications • 1-800-277-8737 • Online! www.superduperinc.com

Game Board 10

Let's Keep the Conversation Going!

Topic Maintenance

Are You on the Topic?

Instructions: Look at the conversation bubbles in each box. If both speakers are on the same topic, color the picture. If the speakers are not on the same topic, put an X on the picture.

Glue-a-Bubble

Instructions: Cut out the conversation bubbles at the bottom of the page. Read the conversation starter in each box. Find an appropriate conversation bubble to continue each conversation. Glue/tape or place each bubble in the correct box.

Let's Keep the Conversation Going!

Name   Homework Partner   Date

#BK-308 Positive Pragmatic Game Boards Fun Sheets • ©2003 Super Duper® Publications • 1-800-277-8737 • Online! www.superduperinc.com

I Love Ice Cream

Instructions: Cut out the ice cream cones and scoops below. Read the conversation parts on each piece. Glue/tape or place the cones onto a separate piece of paper. Then, glue/tape or place in each cone the ice cream scoop that would keep the conversation going.

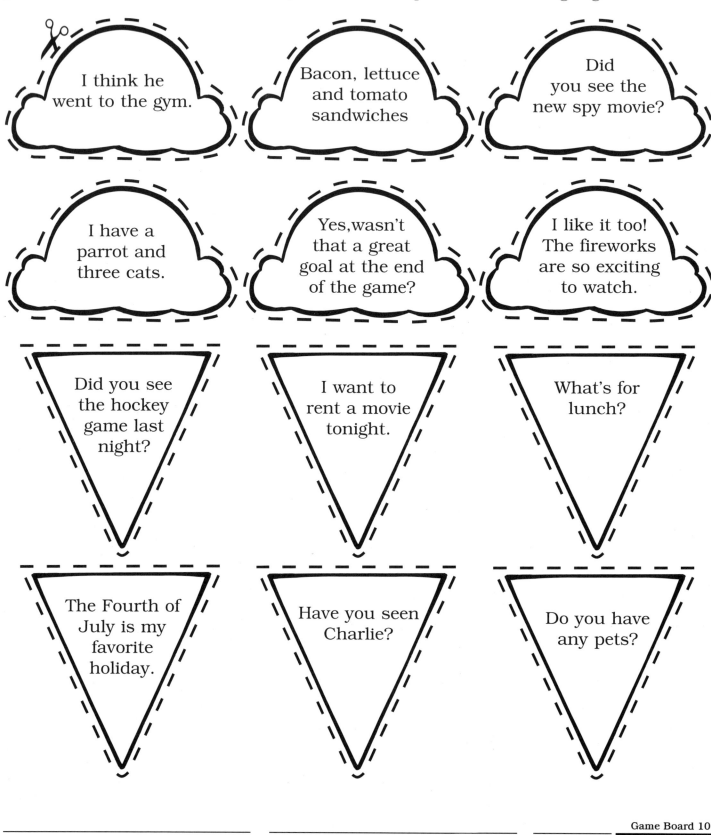

I think he went to the gym.

Bacon, lettuce and tomato sandwiches

Did you see the new spy movie?

I have a parrot and three cats.

Yes, wasn't that a great goal at the end of the game?

I like it too! The fireworks are so exciting to watch.

Did you see the hockey game last night?

I want to rent a movie tonight.

What's for lunch?

The Fourth of July is my favorite holiday.

Have you seen Charlie?

Do you have any pets?

_____
Name

_____
Homework Partner

_____
Date

Game Board 10

Let's Keep the Conversation Going!

#BK-308 Positive Pragmatic Game Boards Fun Sheets • ©2003 Super Duper® Publications • 1-800-277-8737 • Online! www.superduperinc.com

Family Vacation

Instructions: The Smith family is sitting at the dinner table and discussing what they should do on their vacation. Cut out the conversation bubbles below. Five conversation bubbles are on the topic of vacation, while five are not. Glue one vacation bubble above each person in the Smith family. Throw away the five bubbles that do not talk about a vacation.

Can we fly or are we driving?

I love spaghetti.

What's for dinner?

When is Mary going back to college?

Let's go on a fishing trip.

Did you have a good day today?

I would rather go skiing in Colorado.

Will we be away for a week?

I want to go to Disney World.

Can we go to the mall?

_____ _____ _____
Name   Homework Partner   Date

Question Time

Instructions: Read the conversation starter in each box. Answer the conversation starter with a question. Use the question word in the conversation bubble to help get you started.

#BK-308 Positive Pragmatic Game Boards Fun Sheets • ©2003 Super Duper® Publications • 1-800-277-8737 • Online! www.superduperinc.com

Keep It Going

Instructions: Read the conversation starter. Fill in the conversation bubbles to continue the conversation.

Game Board 10

Let's Keep the Conversation Going!

_____   _____   _____

Name   Homework Partner   Date

Conversation Spinner

Instructions: If you prefer, glue this page to construction paper for added durability. Cut out the arrow/dial. Use a brad to connect the dial to the circle. Spin the spinner and continue the conversation the dial lands upon. Keep adding to the conversation. The longer the conversation, the better it is!

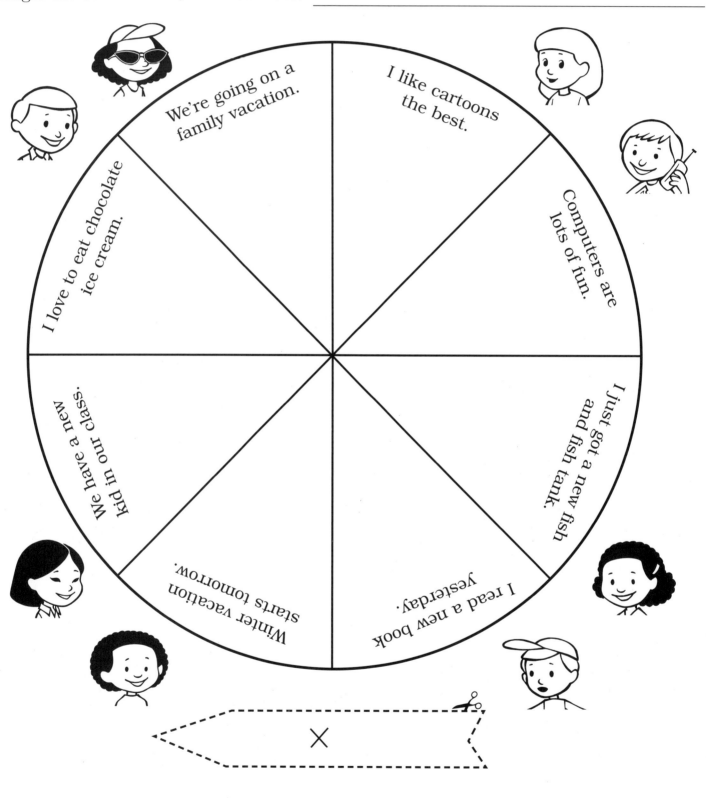

We're going on a family vacation.

I like cartoons the best.

I love to eat chocolate ice cream.

Computers are lots of fun.

We have a new kid in our class.

I just got a new fish and fish tank.

Winter vacation starts tomorrow.

I read a new book yesterday.

✂

×

How Many?

Instructions: If you prefer, glue this page to construction paper for added durability. Cut apart the conversation starter cards and the number cards. Put the conversation starter cards in one pile (Pile A) and the number cards in another pile (Pile B). Player One draws the top card from Pile A. He/she reads the conversation starter. Player Two draws the top card from Pile B and continues the conversation by asking the number of questions indicated on the card. Player One answers the questions. Take turns choosing cards.

This math page is easy.	Tomorrow is my birthday!	We're going on vacation.	We're moving to a new house.
I like cartoons the best.	Computers are fun.	I love chocolate ice cream.	I'm going to a party today.
I just got a new fish.	It's summer vacation.	I read a new book.	I want a new video game.

1	**2**	**2**	**3**
1	**2**	**2**	**3**

✂

Name _____ Homework Partner _____ Date _____

Game Board 10

Let's Keep the Conversation Going!

#BK-308 Positive Pragmatic Game Boards Fun Sheets • ©2003 Super Duper® Publications • 1-800-277-8737 • Online! www.superduperinc.com

Tic-Tac-Toe

Instructions: Cut out the Tic-Tac-Toe markers at the bottom of the page. Player One chooses a box and reads the conversation starter aloud. Player Two responds to the conversation starter. Player One adds one more response to the conversation and places his marker on the box. Player Two chooses a box and reads the conversation starter. Player One responds. Player Two finishes the conversation and places his/her marker on the box. The first player to get three in a row wins!

Have you been to the new ice cream parlor?	What are you doing during your summer vacation?	I got a new bike for my birthday!
I love science!	Do you like going to the beach?	My dog had puppies.
Have you seen my baseball mitt?	I'm going to visit my grandpa on his farm.	I broke my new bike.

_____   _____   _____
Name   Homework Partner   Date

Game Board 10

Let's Keep the Conversation Going!

Good or Bad Communication Skills

Instructions: Look at each picture scene below. Does each picture scene show good communication skills? Look at body language and/or the conversation. If the communication skills are good, color the picture. Put an X on the bad communication skills. Tell what you would do in this situation. _____

Let's Keep the Conversation Going!

_____   _____   _____
Name   Homework Partner   Date

Conversation Game Board

Instructions: Cut out the game markers below. Each player chooses a marker and flips a coin to move around the board. (Heads - move 1 space, Tails - move 2 spaces.) Each player, on his/her turn, should read the conversation starter aloud. Other players take turns adding to the conversation. The original player finishes the conversation he/she started. The next player then takes a turn. The first player to reach the Finish wins.

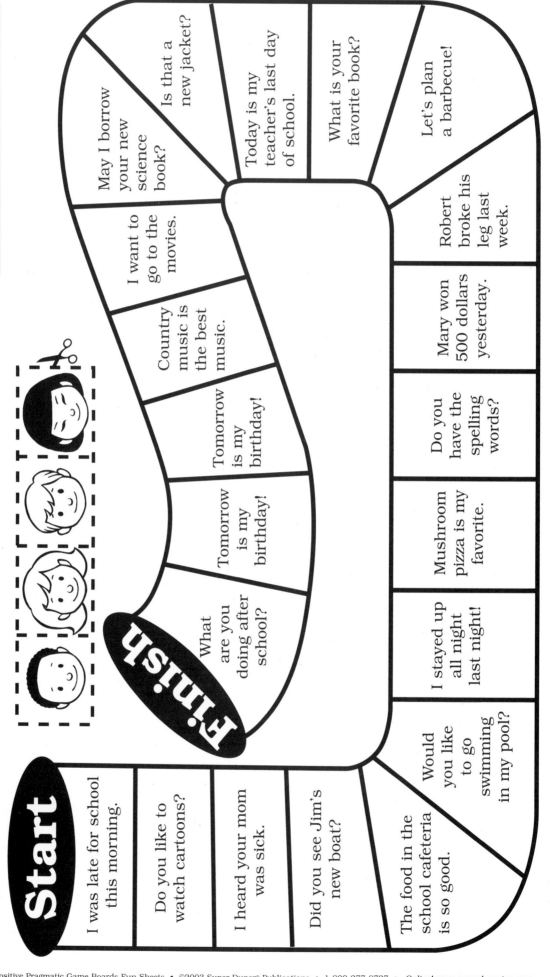

Start

I was late for school this morning.

Do you like to watch cartoons?

I heard your mom was sick.

Did you see Jim's new boat?

The food in the school cafeteria is so good.

Would you like to go swimming in my pool?

I stayed up all night last night!

Mushroom pizza is my favorite.

Do you have the spelling words?

Mary won 500 dollars yesterday.

Robert broke his leg last week.

Let's plan a barbecue!

What is your favorite book?

Today is my teacher's last day of school.

Is that a new jacket?

May I borrow your new science book?

I want to go to the movies.

Country music is the best music.

Tomorrow is my birthday!

Tomorrow is my birthday!

What are you doing after school?

Finish

Game Board 10

Let's Keep the Conversation Going!

Name _____   Homework Partner _____   Date _____

Conversation Wheels

Instructions: Read the conversation starter at the center of each wheel. Try to think of five different ways you could respond to the conversation starter. For example, if the conversation starter is "I feel sick," you could say, "So do I," "What's wrong?" "Did you see a doctor," etc. Draw a line from the conversation starter to each number (starting with one) as you give each response. _____

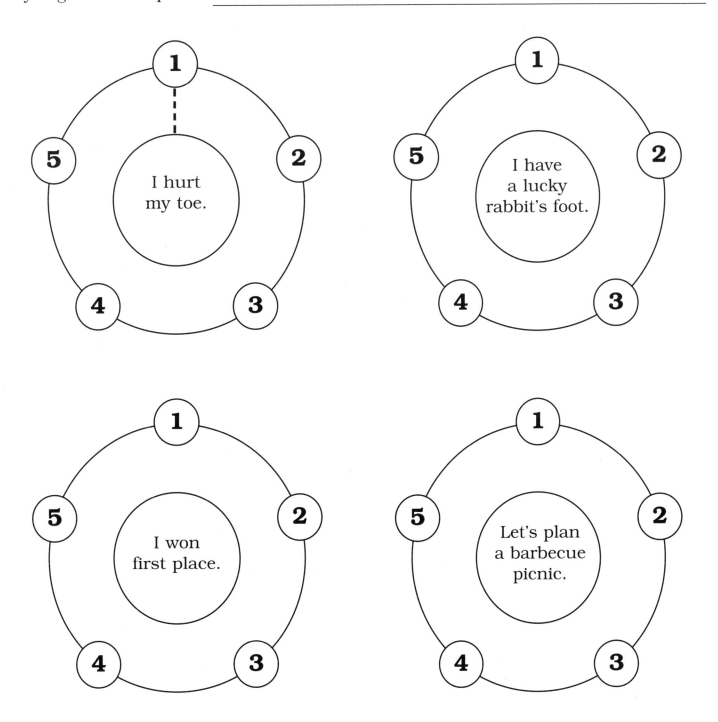

#BK-308 Positive Pragmatic Game Boards Fun Sheets • ©2003 Super Duper® Publications • 1-800-277-8737 • Online! www.superduperinc.com   163

Conversation Connection

Instructions: Read the conversation pieces on each strip. Cut the strips apart along the dotted lines. Make a paper chain starting with the strip that says "I broke my arm." Connect conversation pieces, as links, in order to form a conversation chain. The last link should say, "I hope you feel better."

Glue			Glue
	I broke my arm.		
	Did you go to the hospital?		
	I fell off the slide.		
	Can I sign your cast?		
	Did it hurt?		
	Sure, here's a pen.		
	How did it happen?		
	Yes. They had to put a cast on my arm.		
	It hurt a lot.		
*	I hope you feel better!		*

Carnival Fun

Instructions: Pick a partner and read/listen to the play below. One person will be Jack and the other will be Billy. Read the script aloud. As you read, underline any lines in the play that do not make sense. (Challenge: Try to write a sentence or question that would fit in place of the error.)

Jack: *"I went to a great carnival last night!"*

Billy: *"Where was it?"*

Jack: *"It was in the parking lot down by the firehouse."*

Billy: *"How were the rides?"*

Jack: *"They were great! There was a super fast rollercoaster, a Ferris wheel, and a gigantic octopus ride."*

Billy: *"My little brother went to the movies last night. Did they have any good carnival games?"*

Jack: *"Yes, I won a huge teddy bear at the dart booth. The basketball toss was fun, too!"*

Billy: *"Do you want to watch the baseball game at my house?"*

Jack: *"The food was delicious! The sausage and pepper subs and the cotton candy are my favorites."*

Billy: *"My favorite thing is snowboarding."*

Jack: *"I want to go back to the carnival tonight. Do you want to come with me?"*

Billy: *"I'd love to! I just have to ask my parents."*

Jack: *"Give me a call later and let me know if you can go."*

Billy: *"Okay. I'll see you at school tomorrow."*

_____   _____   _____
Name   Homework Partner   Date

Let's Keep the Conversation Going!

Pass the Mic

Instructions: Glue the page onto construction paper for added durability. Color and cut out the microphone along the dotted line. Use the microphone along with the cards on page 167.

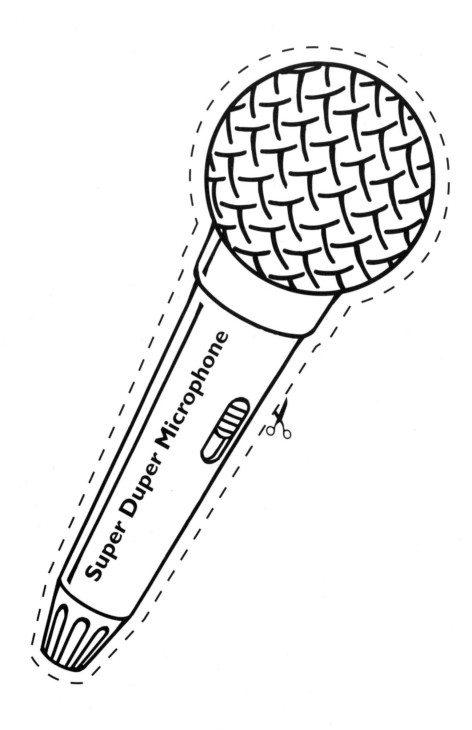

Super Duper Microphone

Name

Homework Partner

Date

Let's Keep the Conversation Going!

Pass the Mic (continued)

Instructions: If you prefer, glue this page onto construction paper for added durability. Cut the cards along the dotted lines. Put all the cards face down on the table. Player One picks up the microphone and chooses a card. Player reads the card to begin the conversation. Player then passes the mic to Player Two to continue the conversation. Player Two answers and gives the mic back to Player One. Players try to keep the conversation going as long as possible. When the conversation ends, the next Player picks a card.

Did you know that tomorrow is my birthday?	I got a new pet.	We're moving to a new house.
I'm going to a party today.	Let's go out for dinner tonight.	My brother is going away to college.
I broke my arm.	My friend is upset with me.	Would you like to start a new club?
I found five dollars in the street.	My pet got sick yesterday.	I don't feel very good.

Game Board 10

_____   _____   _____
Name   Homework Partner   Date

Let's Keep the Conversation Going!

Answer Key

Page 96:   **Across:** 3. confused; 5. angry; 6. happy; 7. sad; 8. disappointed
Down: 1. proud; 2. scared; 4. embarrassed

Page 97:   1. glad; 2. furious; 3. shocked; 4. unhappy; 5. frightened;
6. confused; 7. anxious; 8. alone; 9. envious

Page 114:   1. spill the beans; 2. in hot water; 3. give me a hand; 4. all
thumbs; 5. shake a leg; 6. raining cats and dogs; 7. full of baloney;
8. monkeying around; 9. zip your lips; 10. knock her socks off

_____'s

Social Skills Are Really Improving!

_____   _____

Speech-Language Pathologist   **Date**

Certificate for
Super Social Skills!

_____ has super
social skills in the following areas:

☐ **Giving Information**

☐ **Feelings**

☐ **Persuasion**

☐ **Figurative Language**

☐ **Requesting**

☐ **Appropriate Interaction**

☐ **Telephone Manners**

☐ **Greetings/Politeness**

☐ **Problem Solving**

☐ **Topic Maintenance**

_____   _____
Speech-Language Pathologist   **Date**

Open Ended Race

Instructions: Cut out the game markers below. Flip a coin to determine the number of spaces to move. Heads moves one space. Tails moves two spaces. Take turns moving around the board and completing the task in each square.

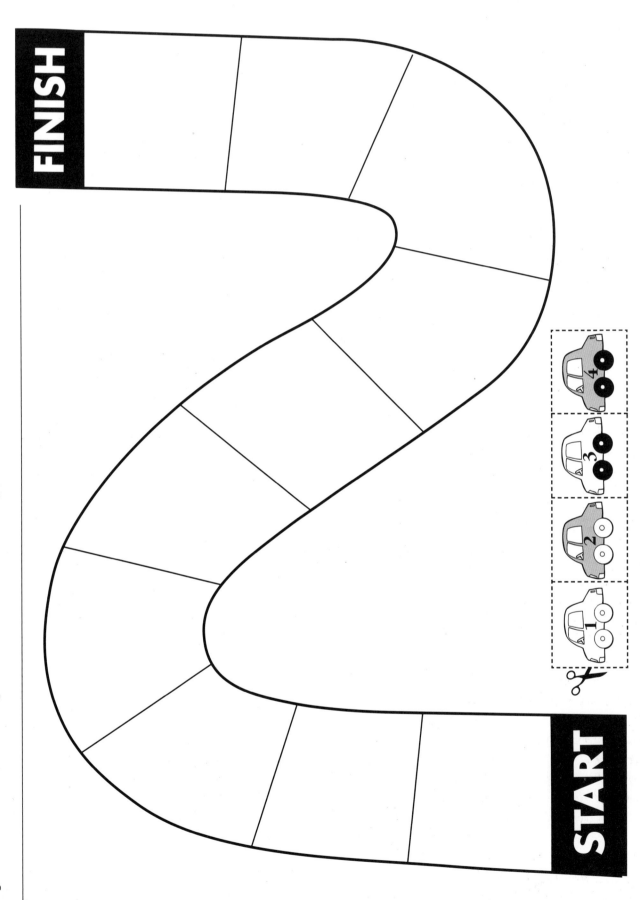

#BK-308 Positive Pragmatic Game Boards Fun Sheets • ©2003 Super Duper® Publications • 1-800-277-8737 • Online! www.superduperinc.com